PLAINS HISTORIES

John R. Wunder, Series Editor

ALSO IN PLAINS HISTORIES

American Outback: The Oklahoma Panhandle in the Twentieth Century, by Richard Lowitt

America's 100th Meridian: A Plains Journey, by Monte Hartman

RAILWAYMAN'S SON

The Rock Island lines, the road most traveled by for the Hawkins family. Adapted from Rock Island timetables, July 1937. Courtesy of H. Roger Grant.

RAILWAYMAN'S SON

A Plains Family Memoir

HUGH HAWKINS

INTRODUCTION BY H. ROGER GRANT

Texas Tech University Press

This book is typeset in Sabon. The paper used in this book meets the minimum requirements of ANSI/NISO Z39.48-1992 (R1997). ∞

Designed by David Timmons

Library of Congress Cataloging-in-Publication Data
Hawkins, Hugh.
Railwayman's son : A Plains family memoir / Hugh Hawkins ; introduction by H. Roger Grant.
    p. cm.—(Plains histories)
    ISBN 0-89672-557-X (hardcover : alk. paper) 1. Hawkins, Hugh—Childhood and youth. 2. Hawkins, Hugh—Family. 3. Goodland (Kan.)—Social life and customs—20th century. 4. Goodland (Kan.)—Biography. 5. El Reno (Okla.)—Social life and customs—20th century. 6. El Reno (Okla.)—Biography. 7. Great Plains—Social life and customs—20th century. 8. Chicago, Rock Island and Pacific Railroad Company 9. Historians—United States—Biography. I. Title. II. Series.
    F689.G6H39 2005
    978.1'033'092—dc22   2005020008

ISBN-13 978-0-89672-557-7

Printed in the United States of America
06 07 08 09 10 11 12 13 14 / 9 8 7 6 5 4 3 2 1
TS

Texas Tech University Press
Box 41037
Lubbock, Texas 79409-1037 USA
800.832.4042
ttup@ttu.edu
www.ttup.ttu.edu

In appreciation of my fellow teachers in an Amherst College course called "Memory": for Alan Babb, David Blight, Peter Czap, Rose Olver, Lisa Raskin, Susan Snively, and in memory of Susan Duffy

Contents

Preface   xi

Introduction by H. Roger Grant   xv

Chapter 1   How We Moved from Herington
            to Goodland   1

Chapter 2   My Brother and My Sisters   14

Chapter 3   Grade School   34

Chapter 4   The Christian Church   47

Chapter 5   My Mother and My Father   56

Chapter 6   Reaching the Rest of the World   65

Chapter 7   At Our House   81

Chapter 8   Where I Wandered   95

Chapter 9   When the Family Traveled   104

Chapter 10 Changed Lives   114

Chapter 11 How We Left Goodland and Saw the
            World of Tomorrow   123

Chapter 12 First Year in a New Town   136

Chapter 13 First Year in a New Town and
            a Bit Beyond   155

Afterword   173

Appendix: The Railwayman Speaks for Himself   181

Acknowledgments   189

Preface

THE YEARS of this memoir belonged to the Great
Depression, one of the more intriguing eras of American
history, and by most definitions Goodland, Kansas,
where I lived from 1935 to 1940, lay in the then-
notorious Dust Bowl. Documentary photographs have
made this region at that time part of Americans' abiding
visual imagery. My memories are not, however, those of a
barefoot child hurrying to a plank shed as clouds of dust
roll in. Although even a secure small-town family worried
about social and natural disasters, only hints of such worries reached me. For me these were years dominated by
relationships within the family, a small social world that I
could observe intently. Gradually I indulged my curiosity
outside the home, in school, in church, and in wanderings
about the town, but public affairs rarely caught my attention. Goodland did not lend itself to lessons about class or
racial distinctions. I learned more about these after we
moved in 1940 to central Oklahoma.

My strongest motivation in writing about the years
before I turned twelve comes from my curiosity about how
memory works. My widowed father in his eighties spent
most of his time in his children's homes, living on for thirteen years after my mother died, in 1968. During the
months he lived with me, I indulged his need to talk,
though the stories grew all too familiar. Almost invariably

they came from his early boyhood: his grandfather's stone house on Badger Crick with its rich variety of apples in the cellar; his regular duty to build the morning fire in his family's farmhouse, which required that he sleep in the loft over the kitchen; and at age twelve his first job with the railroad, working on the roadbed with the section gang. Any reports of later years, except his meeting and marrying my mother, lacked the intensity of those from his earliest memories.

Introspection has shown me a similar skewing of memory. I could tell you a lot about my first day in graduate school, about landing at le Havre on my first trip to Europe, about my unexpected induction into the army. But the surprising memories come from early childhood. (Why had I not thought of that in sixty years? Why should that have been retained at all?)

These recollections have a special freshness, and they are abundant. No one would tolerate a conversation in which I recounted them. Could I record such memories, I asked myself, in a way that anyone else would want to read?

I make no claim to write as a naive recollector. Besides the legendry of public memory, I have internalized the historical context developed by fellow historians. But when broad social developments enter my account here, it is usually because they somehow penetrated childhood's protective shell.

Neither objective nor all-seeing, the innocent eye has the advantage of freedom from adult preconceptions. It is inquisitive, even intrusive. Sometimes meanings come from a proffered explanation, but often they are intuited. From a child's innumerable observations and understandings, why have these memories and not others emerged? Perhaps along the way I can suggest a few answers, though I claim no authority beyond that of introspection. Colleagues in an interdisciplinary course called "Memory," the dedicatees of this book, stimulated my interest in such questions and shared their varied insights into the power and the fallibility of human memory.

If apologies are in order for self-centered writing, I offer them. But without egoistic motives there would have been no book. This is, however, more than a story about me. It tells about family members moving, physically among places and psychologically on a social ladder. The family hoped, or rather believed, that such moves were for the better. As I wrote, I happily found that I cared a great deal about the lives of others, and I have tried to do justice to them as well as to the child I used to be.

Introduction

OR GENERATIONS railroaders and their family members took pride in being associated with a dynamic, vital, even romantic American industry. Whether a track laborer or a trainmaster, being a "railroad man" or connected in some way to this enterprise meant much. Such was the case of J. A. Hawkins, a veteran dispatcher for the Chicago, Rock Island & Pacific Railroad (Rock Island) in Kansas and Oklahoma, and his family, including his younger son, Hugh. *Railwayman's Son* is a unique family memoir of the Great Plains that offers a personal perspective seldom preserved and bountiful information about railroading in the first half of the twentieth century.

The professional career of the senior Hawkins fits nicely the profile of railroad dispatchers, these men (and occasionally women) who directed the passage of trains along a particular operating "division." Hawkins grew up in a farm family and then "went railroadin'." The reasons surely involved financial considerations and prospects for a more exciting life. It became common for thousands of farm lads to find their initial wage-earning experiences with a railroad. After all, this was the first big American industry, and one that employed a massive workforce. When Hawkins "hired out" with the Atchison, Topeka & Santa Fe Railway (Santa Fe) in 1904, railroad employment stood at approximately 1.3 million. In 1920 it peaked at slightly more than 2 million. In the 1920s increased competition from automobiles, buses, and trucks, which operated on an expanding network of all-weather roads, negatively impacted the railroad business, forcing a decline in the workforce. And the Great Depression of the 1930s led to further reductions. In 1933, arguably the most difficult year, fewer than 1 million men and women labored in rail transport, although still a hefty number. The era of World War II, however, significantly increased the railroad workforce, reaching slightly more than 1.4 million in 1945. Being a railroader usually meant steady work, once an individual gained ample seniority, generally excellent wages, particularly if employment were outside the South, access to inexpensive medical care, free or reduced rates for rail travel, and other benefits. Moreover, railroading, for a farm boy like Hawkins, was far more interesting than the daily, seasonal, and yearly routines of agriculture. Every day was different with a railroad job that directly involved operations, and in Hawkins's case learning the mysteries of the cryptic Morse code became a worthy personal accomplishment and a badge of pride. Starting his career as a relief operator on the "extra board" meant considerable traveling, adding perhaps to the attractiveness of railroad work for a young, unattached male. "In eighteen months," noted the senior Hawkins, "I worked at sixteen different stations on the Eastern Division [of the Santa Fe]." He then followed the established career path by becoming in 1907 a permanent depot agent in a small station. At that point his employer, though, was the Rock Island rather than the Santa Fe. It was common for an agent-operator to move from carrier to carrier. In fact, there was a "boomer" class of telegraphers who during their careers might find employment on a dozen or more roads. Once a person learned bookkeeping, operating rules, and telegraphy, job options existed, and all without the need for much formal education. In the case of Hawkins, it was the seventh grade, which was typical for the period.

Unlike most agent-operators, Hawkins did not follow the ladder upward in station service. He knew that in time he could bid on a better-paying and -situated job on the Rock Island or for that matter on any other carrier. Based on seniority, job performance, and luck, a capable agent eventually might win assignment to a major terminal and assume a supervisory role. Yet Hawkins and fellow agent-operators had the option of entering another level by becoming a train dispatcher and ultimately a chief dispatcher. Virtually every train dispatcher came from the ranks of agent-operators or towermen.

Further comments made by son Hugh about his father's career as a dispatcher fit the norm. There was job movement: first, Herington, Kansas, then Goodland, Kansas, and finally El Reno, Oklahoma. All of these communities, particularly El Reno, were "Rock Island towns." As such they resembled scores of such places throughout America, including the Great Plains. It might be Denison, Texas (Missouri-Kansas-Texas); Huron, South Dakota (Chicago & North Western); Pittsburg, Kansas (Kansas City Southern) or Wymore, Nebraska (Burlington Route), all closely associated with a single carrier. And then there was the strain of dispatching. The senior Hawkins suffered from ulcer attacks, eye strain, and at times disrupted sleep patterns, being required as a dispatcher to work the third "trick" from midnight to 8 A.M. Likely, too, there were other effects of a usually stressful job. After all, if the dispatcher misjudged train movements, a "cornfield meet" might occur, with equipment damage, personal injuries, and possibly deaths. Such a tragic event could result in a dispatcher's suspension, demotion, or dismissal. Criminal prosecution might also be a consequence.

Men who worked as agent-operators and train dispatchers often shared additional characteristics. Railroaders in the region were likely to be Protestants and Masons. Hawkins was a member of the Disciples of Christ (Christian Church) and he was a Mason. Although a regular churchgoer, he was not too active with this fraternal order. The Rock Island was long considered a "Protestant" railroad. It was also common for Rock Island employees, especially train crews and office personnel, to join the Masonic Order; in some instances membership was essential for advancement in the job place. Considering religion and fraternal connections, it is not surprising that most agents and dispatchers lacked any real tradition of labor radicalism. Members of the Order of Railroad Telegraphers and the American Train Dispatchers Association tended to be conservative. Hawkins represents this outlook, although he did express admiration for Eugene Victor Debs, leader of the locomotive firemen's union, founder of the industrial American Railway Union, and perennial Socialist Party candidate for president.

Although Hawkins left the robust Santa Fe for the not-so-mighty Rock Island, he did not necessarily make a foolish career change. The company was a major "Class 1" and operated in modern, sophisticated fashion. Though the Santa Fe had its financial ups and downs in the twentieth century, it evolved into one of America's best railroads. The saga of the Rock Island, however, was less stellar, with the company entering bankruptcy in 1915, 1933, and 1975. Yet the Rock Island did not become a financial basket case and a transportation slum until after Hawkins had retired, finally being liquidated in the early 1980s.

In the 1930s the Rock Island sprawled for nearly eight thousand miles across fourteen states from the Midwest into the South, West, and Southwest. Its network of lines served such major centers as Chicago, Dallas, Denver, Des Moines, Kansas City, Memphis, Minneapolis-St. Paul,

Oklahoma City, Omaha, and St. Louis, although the company often found itself in the least competitive position. And that perpetually caused financial difficulties.

In 1933 the Rock Island entered its second bankruptcy, and it did not exit from court control until 1948. Although these were years of struggle, the company benefited from strong corporate leadership. In 1936 the road's receivers turned to the able John Dow Farrington, general manager of Burlington Route affiliate Fort Worth & Denver City Railway, to take charge. When Farrington assumed his presidential duties, he discovered that maintenance had long been deferred, motive power and rolling stock needed to be replaced and updated, and the bureaucracy required attention. Indeed, Farrington and his talented, dedicated management team would be responsible for consolidating the dispatching offices, resulting in the closing of the Goodland facility and explaining why the Hawkins family relocated to El Reno.

Farrington became a well-liked and effective officer. Hugh Hawkins remembered, "[Dad] spoke confidently of reorganization and of 'Farrington,' the new man at the top." Without question Farrington rehabilitated the property, and in the process introduced snappy, streamlined passenger trains, which pleased patrons and boosted company morale. These new trains, which the Rock Island called *Rockets*, came a few years after the Burlington and Union Pacific had grabbed national, even international, attention for their diesel-powered, stainless steel, high-speed *Zephyrs* and *Cities* streamliners. The first Rock Island *Rocket* run, between Chicago and Peoria, Illinois, had the desired effect: passenger revenue on the line increased. The company added similar trains to other cities, including Colorado Springs and Denver, and they raced through the towns and villages of the Great Plains. These state-of-the-art name trains, plus improved maintenance, acquisition of

diesel-powered yard and road locomotives, and other bet-
terments, resulted in heightened revenues and helped to
bring about a successful reorganization. Moreover,
employees, including the senior Hawkins, were immensely
proud of these new trains, and, as his son notes, "Much of
the town turned out to see the *Rocky Mountain Rocket* on
its initial run through Goodland in November 1939."

For dispatcher Hawkins work became more hectic with
the outbreak of World War II. El Reno was a strategic point
on the Rock Island system, with lines radiating to Memphis
to the east, Tucumcari, New Mexico, to the west, Herington and Kansas City to the north, and Dallas and the Gulf
Coast to the south. Wartime traffic, both freight and passenger, accelerated to record volumes. It was typical for
every employee who was directly involved in train movements and track and equipment maintenance to labor long
hours. Hawkins, according to his son, "rarely got his day
off and frequently worked overtime." This was a dramatically different scenario from the Depression and Dust Bowl
years of the 1930s.

As a testimonial to the attractive pay received by more
senior agents and dispatchers, the Hawkins family by the
1930s achieved a relatively good lifestyle. The family
owned what contemporaries usually considered to be lux-
ury automobiles, acquiring, for example, a 1936 Chrysler.
And, thanks in part to "trip passes," the family was able to
attend the popular World's Fair in New York City and
make extended visits elsewhere, including the West Coast.
And when the Hawkinses moved to El Reno, they acquired
one of the better houses.

What *Railwayman's Son* reveals is a family that mostly
prospered due to the dedicated efforts of a skilled, hardworking agent-operator father turned dispatcher. Although
every family unit is unique, the impact of railroad employment represents that of thousands of other men who pur-

sued like work. The Rock Island, though hardly a money machine, enabled the Hawkinses to enjoy a comfortable life in small-town Kansas and Oklahoma. Later, however, Rock Island men and women had a different experience. When the railroad first failed to merge with the mighty Union Pacific in the 1960s in what became the most controversial rail merger case of the era, and then fell apart in 1980 and 1981, thousands of loyal workers lost their jobs permanently. They had to either find work with other carriers or businesses, or take retirement. In the process the town of El Reno suffered also. When the family moved there in 1940, the senior Hawkins believed that "the dispatcher's office there could never be abolished." He was correct for his railroading career, but ultimately there were no Rock Island trains to dispatch, and the facility closed forever. The Rock Island failed to find a corporate home in the rapidly consolidating world of American railroading and became a "fallen flag" carrier.

H. ROGER GRANT
CLEMSON UNIVERSITY

Railwayman's Son

CHAPTER 1

How We Moved from Herington to Goodland

Goodland . . . (3,687 alt., 3,626 pop.) is a modern western county seat, with a few attractive office buildings, a railroad division office quarters, and a modern courthouse, ranged along a wide main street.

—*The WPA Guide to 1930s Kansas* (1939), p. 335

MOVING to Goodland did not win my approval. But what did a seven-year-old have to say in so momentous a family decision? A family is not a democracy, as my mother once said. The goal was to have us all live where my father worked. The Rock Island railroad (officially the "Chicago, Rock Island, & Pacific") was consolidating its dispatchers' offices, and the one in Herington had been closed. My father had been transferred to Goodland, far to the west, barely inside Kansas. There were no hills there, and nobody had yet romanticized it as "Big Sky Country." The only trees in sight seemed to be a few struggling Chinese elms. Worst of all, Goodland lay in the Dust Bowl.

In Herington I had been happy in the first grade at Lincoln School, something of a pet to Miss Zarnowski, perhaps because I wasn't intimidated by her name. In September 1936 I had begun the second grade and was even more in love with the new teacher. But a week after school started the decision was made. Perhaps I was forewarned, but all I remember is waking up one morning to find my clothes packed and an early departure scheduled.

When I protested that all my new schoolbooks were in my desk at school, I was assured that Daddy had gone there with the principal the night before and picked them up. How little the grown-ups knew. Our beautiful colored construction paper had been gathered into a locked cabinet for safekeeping. The principal hadn't known about that.

This family uprooting sprang out of the Great Depression. I have no recollection of the word "depression" being used to explain our displacement, whose source lay rather in an ominous "consolidation." After good times returned, when my mother's friends were comparing their troubles in the 1930s, a time when they had tried to make do as jobs were lost and income dwindled, she would join the lamentation. "Jim was never out of work, but we did have to leave our home and move all the way out to Goodland." Yes, we too had suffered.

On the day of my birth, September 3, 1929, the stock market had peaked before its unrelenting, disastrous decline set in. In fact, my very conception around Christmastime 1928 may reflect the culmination of the business-admiring overconfidence of the Coolidge era.

Yet even in the 1920s the railroads had been a sick industry. Automobiles and trucks and better highways had undercut the nation's reliance on rail transportation, whose earlier dominance had made it such a good choice when my father was finding his occupation.

The most dispiriting part of the Depression had passed by the time my memories set in. But it is easy to imagine the fears of a family, with all five children still at home, whose one wage earner worked in a declining enterprise. In later years, when her historian son inquired, Mother recalled

With 1920s prosperity, a new baby (the last) and a new car (the first) seemed reasonable. Author's collection.

that she had voted for Franklin D. Roosevelt—once, in 1932. This departure from the family's traditional Republicanism told a lot about shattered foundations of faith. By 1936 my parents were back in the fold, supporting their fellow Kansan, Alf Landon. To no avail, of course, in the face of FDR's landslide.

Landon's candidacy lets me date one early memory. On July 23, 1936, I was in Topeka watching a parade. It was Notification Day, celebrating an archaic ceremony that let Governor Landon know he had been nominated for president. Since this was hardly news, he could respond with an elaborate acceptance speech. The prospect of the parade excited me. Mostly, however, I remember heat and thirst, intensifying the frustration of a view blocked by a taller child in front of me. But there is more—a wealth of bright yellow sunflower badges and the rhymed slogan "Save your socks for Landon and Knox." Plus something terrible, news that a man in the crowd had been crushed by an elephant from the parade. Or did my sister Rena just make that up to scare me?

I heard a lot of talk about how bad things were for the farmers. Of my mother's family, one brother and one sister were still farming near Topeka, though that brother relied on carpentry as much as farming. Unable to pay the mortgage, my father's family had been willing to let the bank take the old family farm, which they had rented out. To prevent that humiliation, Dad used his savings to intervene, insisting that the farm now be held in his name. His siblings had moved into town. For them, farm life became the nostalgia of childhood, not a continuing personal reality. Emporia, once the market for the family's truck gardening, was now home.

When pressed to jog her memory about our relocation, my sister Rena recalls a dinner-table conversation in which

Mother imagined how she might earn money. She could open a restaurant in our Herington home, conveniently situated on a national highway, or even return to the land and raise chickens. I can only guess how much these fantasies expressed frustrated entrepreneurial drive (Mother took pride in her managerial skills) and how much genuine concern that Dad might fail as the family breadwinner.

Strangely enough, I had lived in Goodland once before. In 1934–35, when I was only five, we had found a renter for our Herington house and had ourselves rented a house on Cherry Street in Goodland. The return to Herington in mid-1935 included only Mother and the two youngest children, my sister Rena, aged ten, and me, just turning six on the day school started.

My father remained in Goodland with my brother, Dean, eighteen years older than I was, and the third child, Ruth, just entering high school. Dean had found a job there as a bookkeeper, and Ruth, aware that the whole family would ultimately move to Goodland, wanted to have all her high school education in one place. The oldest of the three girls, Helene, was away at college that year.

This return was, so far as I can reconstruct the situation, related to the departure of our undesirable tenants and perhaps a wish to preserve our Herington roots. It was here that my father had advanced his career by "breaking in" as a dispatcher. Here my parents had entered wholeheartedly into club life and seen their older children become leading school citizens.

Dad took pains not to neglect the Herington branch of the family. Far away though Goodland was, he could travel free on the rail lines between the two towns. He had a pass, of course, but rarely showed it since he knew every conductor along the way. Making arrangements with a dispatcher who had been laid off, Dad could combine his "day off" with a second day or more while this substitute covered for him. Sometimes on these hurried visits he brought one of the Goodland-based children with him.

Nothing particular during my 1934–35 life in Goodland had turned me against the town. It just wasn't really home. I knew we still owned our house in Herington and could not imagine that we would ever sell it. (Indeed, my parents kept it as long as they lived, finding in it some special security.)

It meant nothing to me that the house we rented on Cherry Street was considerably newer than the one we owned. Abundant bright polished pinewood gave a glow to the interior, and the high front porch boasted a railing of open brickwork. The street was not paved, but then few were in Goodland. One cloudburst, a rarity in that era of drought, left a huge puddle at the corner. I was allowed, even encouraged, to go wading in the mixture of water, mud, and sand, and was forgiven for getting my clothes wet. Rain was a blessing that invited indulgence.

The Cherry Street house had a serious drawback, however. The basement rooms were rented to another family, the Timms. Although my parents had briefly lived with Mother's mother in Topeka after their marriage in 1910, they had never shared a residence with strangers. If there was a Mr. Timm, I do not remember him. But the daughter, perhaps about seven years old, proved a good playmate, nearer my own age and less bossy than my sister Rena. In fact I was a little in love with Louise.

My affection for her did not, however, prevent a quarrel over the outcome of a backyard game. I won a brief emotional victory by announcing, "Your mother is nothing but a gossip." This was of course repetition of a comment of my mother's when she had warned us not to share family affairs with the Timms. Louise crumpled in tears, and Rena hastened to report my slander. I was sternly instructed to keep private not only family affairs, but family opinions of other people.

A second calamity was physical. Louise had joined Rena and me on the front porch with its pretty open brick balustrades, topped with cement ledges. We had made up. After all, she was good company. She perched on the railing as we exchanged banter. After one of her own jokes, she threw back her head to laugh, her balance shifted, and the cement ledge, its bonding inadequate to the challenge, slid off. Over she went, dropping headfirst to the ground some five feet below. I was paralyzed. Rena ran for help. As I watched in horror, Mother stretched Louise out on our davenport, applying cold compresses to her head and body. Life, it seemed, was a risky affair.

Louise recovered quickly, and before long the Timms moved out. We took over the basement, even though it meant a higher rent.

My other memorable companion, Winifred, lived a block away and across the street. I played happily with her at her house, sometimes at ours. Her little sister Jenny wasn't so much fun, but sometimes we included her in our games.

A conspicuous feature of Winifred's backyard was a disused chicken house. Neatly constructed, it had one door, many windows, and perches for the chickens, whose lumpy droppings attested still to their former residence.

One afternoon, bored with our usual games, I suggested using the poultry sanctum for a new adventure. I didn't propose to play doctor, just to go in and take off our clothes. This Winifred and I proceeded to do. For privacy we had Jenny hook the door. The hook was on the outside, but this security lapse escaped my attention. Then, hoping to widen the excitement, I proposed that Jenny join us by climbing through a window.

The windows did not open very wide, and Jenny could only get through legs first, up to her navel. This was a disappointment, but I did what I could, urging Winifred to join me in rubbing Jenny's tummy, chanting, "Isn't that soft and round!" The younger sister offered no objection, eager as ever to be tolerated in our fun. Differences in genitals were of no interest so far as I recall. The joy lay in sharing the forbidden freedom from clothing.

Perhaps spotting Jenny's squirming torso, the girls' mother came out of the house, unlatched the coop door, and helped us get back into our clothes. At least she helped Winifred. I quickly redressed myself. I felt guilty, which should be interpreted as meaning that I feared my folks at home would be told. Winifred's mother did not reprimand me, but her advice that I had better go home found me more than willing. No observable consequences followed. The girls and I did play together again, though never so creatively.

It was not misadventures with little girls that made me prefer Herington to Goodland. The Herington years had been happy ones, both in their dailiness and in incidents that stayed in my memory. There we lived in "our house." Our Herington address 401 South C Street, the first I ever learned by heart, rang through my head like a chant, a bit of music that assured safety and identity. This Dutch colonial (the proper architectural label for which I learned some years later) stood on a corner at the top of the steepest hill in town. By its side ran the Old Santa Fe Trail, important in history, I was told, and now a major highway. Enough out-of-state cars passed to show that Herington counted for something.

We lived only a block from Lincoln School, easy to walk to, safe with or without Rena. I preferred walking with my buddy W. T. Zabell, who lived at the bottom of our hill. For my seventh birthday, he gave me a neatly inscribed Big-

*401 South C Street. Herington had snowfalls, but never the bliz-
zards, white and black, that beset Goodland. Author's
collection.*

Little book. With the help of its generous illustration, I
could grasp Little Lord Fauntleroy's dilemma, and its mul-
tiple pictures of Freddie Bartholomew proved that even at
our young age one could become a movie star. I felt ambi-
tion stirring, goals for which my father's career offered no
apparent model.

Near W. T.'s house rose the standpipe. This silver water
tower was the highest structure in town and its guarantor
of water pressure. Though in awe of this piece of engineer-
ing, it never occurred to me to fear it. But apparently others were less secure. One day Miss Zarnowski felt obliged
to puncture rumors that the standpipe could fall on us. Of
course I knew she was right, and from then on I viewed the
looming eminence with even greater respect—as an intim-
idator of the credulous.

401 South C was part of a neighborhood in a way that our Goodland residences never became. We could name every family up and down our block, and the younger folks moved easily in and out of neighbors' houses. The Jakeys were the only exception. A childless couple, they erected a brick wall around their yard, and we shared scare stories of what they might do to anyone caught inside.

One day I joined two neighborhood boys in scaling the wall. We dropped into the Jakeys' tidy yard and stared at the drawn blinds of their windows. Who knew what lay behind them? I felt trapped. Heart beating wildly, at the risk of being called a coward, I urged that we climb back out. Though the others admitted no fear, my plea provided the excuse for a general retreat.

A very different neighbor, everyone's "Auntie" Dayton, lived in the big house next door to us, separated by a hedge of roses. Both families picked the blossoms, though the bushes had been planted on her side before spreading. Once, little helper that I was, I plucked a rose from the Dayton side for a bouquet Mother was gathering. This was a transgression, and she firmly instructed me to replace it by giving Auntie Dayton a rose from our side. The Hawkinses were very strict about property rights.

Across the street lived Florence, a distant relative of the Daytons, who had been raised by them after she was orphaned. I visited her house as often as possible, particularly at mealtimes. Feeding me some Campbell's alphabet soup, Florence encouraged me to name each letter in the spoonful before swallowing it.

One day I strolled into Florence's kitchen with a bit of yellow yolk dried on my upper lip.

"I know what you had for breakfast today!"

"What?"

"Eggs."

"Oh, no. I had that yesterday."

The resulting hilarity excited me, and the begged-for explanation of what was funny made me feel not naïve, but rather witty. Despite our usual sensitivity to what the neighbors might say, this incident became a family in-joke. In my first appearance onstage, with yellow chalk smeared across my mouth, I reenacted the scene for a high school variety show, scripted by my sister Helene. Laughter and applause rose from the darkened auditorium, and I left the stage elated.

In the evenings as many as a dozen children, ages four to fifteen, might be playing up and down the sidewalks and on the generous grassed area between sidewalk and curbing that we called "the parking." For kick-the-can we played right in the middle of the street. I could stay until it grew dark, waiting till I heard the metallic clacker Mother used to call us in.

If we played in our own front yard, we could stay out even after dark. Along the front porch, just high enough for a convenient perch, a bevy of Hawkins children and their friends would gather, numbers dwindling as the evening wore on. Once when, in the failing light, I tripped and struck my forehead on the edge of the porch, others called the adults, who found me bleeding and in tears. The loving attention and the sting of the disinfectant brought reassurance, and the resulting scar provided a great bragging point. I rather regretted its early disappearance beneath my growing eyebrow.

Most evenings ended less dramatically. With only mild urging, Helene would launch into the creepy tale that began, "It was a dark and stormy night on the plains of Arizona, when someone rose and said, 'Abbie, tell us a story,' and Abbie rose and said, 'It was a dark and stormy night on the plains of Arizona, when someone rose and said . . .'" And so onward into an infinite loop, broken only because a hypnotic drowsiness made me happy to be led indoors.

Hunting Easter eggs, a once-a-year treat, followed an exciting two days of dyeing and decorating the hardboiled eggs. But it was no fun if older children found them all. During the first hunt I can recall, I wandered about a long time with nothing to put in my basket. In a bit of sisterly conspiracy, Ruth showed me where some of the prettiest eggs had been hidden. When I displayed them to the group, I was challenged.

"You didn't find those by yourself."

"I did too!"

The accusation and the lie, not the joy of possession, made the occasion memorable.

Although too young to participate, I could still watch the magical game of "Heavy heavy hangs over thy head," a variant of the better-known twenty questions. Following this ominous incantation, the blindfolded contestant asked the set first question, "Fine or superfine?" with the answer providing the initial clue, the gender of the object's owner. That it was girls who were superfine raised no objections, fitting neatly with the principle "Ladies first."

I had no doubt that Elizabeth Tripp was superfine. My favorite neighborhood playmate, she was five years older, the same age as Rena. Just to be tolerated as her companion was an honor, but she even took me up in her tree house and showed me her treasures, including a dented shiny coffee pot that functioned as a mirror.

It was at Elizabeth's house that I had lost my baby ring, a gift from one of our aunts. My sisters had carried me up there with the ill-fitting bit of jewelry on my one-year-old finger. It is only the happy outcome that I remember. One day when I was nearly six, Elizabeth's brother arrived jauntily carrying the ring on a twig. While he was raking leaves, the ring had slid onto a rake tine, rejecting the world of nature for the civilized realm. This tiny circlet excited me, talismanic proof that I had a personal history, one that involved risk and loss and redemption. The ring joined other family heirlooms in Mother's small silver jewelry box, and the tale of its return joined the family stock of strange and wonderful occurrences.

No such legends linked us to the western Kansas town that now laid claim to be our home.

My Brother and My Sisters

IN MY EARLY MEMORIES my brother and my three sisters appear not only as individuals with distinctive traits, but also sometimes in vivid scenes, occasionally including their very words. Some of these moments have come to mind repeatedly over the years, but others mysteriously reappeared when I began to dwell on my family's life during my childhood. The self I recall tends to be the one my siblings reacted to: for all of them a responsibility, but sometimes the "darling little brother," as Helene's diary put it, and sometimes the little pest.

Dean: The Enigma

I would have been an Eagle Scout if I hadn't had to
stay home and change your diapers.
—Dean

Growing up the youngest of five brought me lots of moral instruction. My siblings joined my parents in pointing out right and wrong. After all, born in 1911, 1915, 1920, and 1924, they felt free, even obliged, to teach the latecomer of 1929. Rena's advice had the advantage of her closeness in age, but given our competitiveness, she sometimes exaggerated my failings. Dean, the eldest, was the most reticent, but I paid attention when he expressed his views, even if only by gesture. I could never quite figure him out. His sardonic declaration that taking care of me had frus-

Having all five Hawkins children in one picture was rare, perhaps because of the eighteen-year age spread. Here, in 1930, back row: Dean and Helene holding Hugh; front row: Ruth and Rena. The recently purchased Marquette is behind us. Author's collection.

trated his scouting ambitions indicated something close to resentment.

For the most part, Dean seemed as much an adult as my parents, and it never occurred to me to wonder why he had not left home. I thought of him, as—like the rest of the family—available for my comfort, instruction, and entertainment, though I did recognize the prematurely deep frown lines above his nose and the sour smell that warned of irritation. At times the irritation came from my eagerness for games, especially verbal ones. As a five-year-old, I delighted in this exchange:

"What's your name?"

"John Brown. Ask me again and I'll knock you down."

Once in the living room, when I interrupted his reading by posing the question with exasperating persistence, Dean did shove me to the floor. With manipulative cunning, I pretended to be hurt and even faked a sob or two. This brought the desired remorse, but also the peculiar odor of his frustration.

On Goodland's Main Street one afternoon, Mother, Dean, and I waited in our Chrysler in front of Duckwall's five-and-dime while Ruth ran an errand. Gladys Adams, an eligible young woman belonging, like us, to the Christian Church, came out of the store. She smiled in our direction. Mother nodded. After Miss Adams passed on by, Mother chided Dean, "You ought to tip your hat to a lady."

He growled back, "I'll tip my hat to a lady, but not to a nightowl." Mother fell silent. I didn't ponder the implications, but something—perhaps the sharp antithesis or startling metaphor—made the phrase unforgettable.

On another occasion, as he took the driver's seat and readjusted the rearview mirror, he informed his little brother that it was almost impossible to reset the mirror after some woman putting on her lipstick had "had a whack at it."

A skillful driver, Dean installed a knob on the steering wheel that allowed driving with one hand. School-day afternoons, when a big dust storm threatened, there was my brother to drive me home, one hand on the plastic knob. The family relied on Dean's ability to identify every car on the road by make and year. As soon as ads for the new models appeared in the *Saturday Evening Post*, he would cut out pictures of the glamorous new products and file them.

Before I was born, when Dean was the only son, he and my father had shared mechanical adventures. Indications lay about the house. Why did the Belgian rug have a hole in it, making it suitable only to be used as a pad below another rug? Because, Mother explained with a barely suppressed sigh, Dad and Dean had spilled battery acid on it when building the family's first radio. Although I never heard that radio, its walnut case remained in use as a small cabinet, and its cast iron loudspeaker had become a lamp base, regularly repainted as one sister after another adapted it to the décor of her room. Such relics of father-son collaboration stirred my wondering admiration. No such ventures linked me to my father, now well into his forties with responsibilities for five children.

One evening as we drove home in the twilight of a late Goodland summer, the subject of my approaching birthday arose. "How old will you be now?" Dean asked.

"Eight," I answered proudly.

He didn't even pause before issuing his warning. "Well, you're going to find that your life is a lot harder from now on."

What could he mean? Why would he say that? There had been disappointments in his life, most then unknown to me, but had they started at age eight? And were they so many that he had forsaken all plans to strike out on his own? The remark stayed with me, becoming something of a consolation when anything bad happened. Just as Dean predicted, I would say to myself.

Dean arrived in Goodland without a job, but soon found one at a modest salary managing the paperwork for the O. K. Packing Company, the euphemistically named local slaughterhouse. No one expected him to land as stable a job as my father's, protected by his often-mentioned "seniority." In those Depression years many sons in their mid-twenties were living at home. Still, in retrospect I wonder how I could have taken Dean's presence for granted, and I understand his gloominess. He was not a liberated adult, but a member of his father's family, valued and useful, but feeling trapped.

As I later learned, upon graduation from high school Dean received a scholarship to Emporia Business College, a school owned by my father's older brother Earl. This uncle vigorously espoused the dominant business ideology of the 1920s, seeing in the so-called New Era a perpetual growth machine. Dean boarded in Emporia with Dad's family, his sweet-tempered widowed mother and the three of her seven children still at home. His first letter after arrival in June 1930 dutifully reported cutting his book bill to $9.10, getting a 95 on his first bookkeeping assignment, and not having time to be homesick. A year later he was fully trained in typing, rapid calculation, and general bookkeeping.

Then he entered Washburn College in Topeka, home of most of Mother's family. Living with Mother's mother, the matriarchal Grandmother Eddy, he completed the school year, but then something went drastically wrong. Years later he told me of his realization that it wasn't after all so very important for him to become a history teacher, a goal he had set even before leaving high school. Shocked to learn that he had hoped to follow the occupation that I later entered, I began to ponder the large roles of luck and timing in life trajectories.

One day in Goodland, as I sat watching Dean turn the pages of a magazine looking for automobile ads, he spotted the arch face of a model promoting Real Silk hosiery. "Yeah, I once tried to sell some of that," he said. This was news to me. In fact, while a freshman at Washburn Dean had been recruited as a summer salesman for that company.

Only long after did I learn more of the story from my father. Dad had been uneasy when he visited Dean at the company's training program. The young men were furiously practicing their sales techniques on each other, gesticulating frenetically and scarcely pausing for breath. Then when Dean came home for his first break, he went about the neighborhood trying to convince others, like the Tripp brothers, to become Real Silk salesmen. It seemed clear to my parents that he was suffering some sort of mania, in their terminology no doubt "a nervous breakdown." They consulted a doctor friend, and though they were willing to send Dean to the private Menninger Clinic in Topeka, the doctor advised that Dean would have as good a chance for recovery at the free state mental hospital in the same city.

For several weeks my father went up on the train from Herington each day after finishing his "trick"—his eight-hour stint as a dispatcher—and would walk about the hospital grounds with Dean. The upshot of this and other counseling was that Dean could come home, having learned "not to take himself so seriously" and, as family parlance had it, "not to overdo." The more I learned, the better I understood Dean's vinegary manner in the Goodland years, quite different, Helene told me after Dean's death in 1952, from the boisterous adolescent she had grown up with.

In my family, chemical change in the brain explained nothing about mental illness. One had to seek a source in the environment. I heard three different theories about Dean's case. My father blamed the "nervous breakdown" on Real Silk pressures. My mother was sure Dean had not been given a healthy diet while living with my father's family in Emporia. Helene thought Washburn and the different sexual standards there (she mentioned mannish women professors) had precipitated the crisis.

Because Dean's travail occurred during my babyhood, I grew up with a much older brother present in my life. I only half-recognized his grim adjustment to parental control, but I saw enough to make sure later of my own freedom. Still, during all my years at home, I was treated leniently, even cosseted. I suspect my parents had concluded that too stringent demands on a child can prove costly. Sometimes they warned me to "relax and get plenty of rest."

Helene: The Surrogate Mother

I'd rather burn out than rust out.

—Helene

Helene's life diverged sharply from Dean's. Her diaries from the 1930s reveal a highly organized, articulate young woman. Surviving photographs show her and her best friend, Lela Edlin, clowning with their tennis rackets. The black-and-white snapshots could not capture the honey color of her hair or the warmth of her green eyes, projecting a self-confident generosity toward the world. From Herington days I can remember visits at the house by her high school boyfriends, especially the affable redhead "Punkin." Spread on the upright piano in the living room, her sheet music featured voluptuous flappers and breezy college boys. Some covers announced the inclusion of ukulele accompaniment.

On a summer auto trip with two female cousins and her very young little brother, Helene led the singing and tossed her apple core into a hayfield. Admonished (by me?) for throwing things from the car window, she lightheartedly defended returning to nature what was nature's own. A little later she pulled the car over near a tempting pond. In the shelter of some trees, we took off our clothes, and though I could not swim we all waded in. The girls demonstrated various swim strokes, and I recall the sensual satisfaction of being held safe against Helene's floating breasts.

After she left for college, she came home for weekends accompanied by fascinating friends. Her chum Ellen Towse brought so many shoes along that even years later Mother would recall her revulsion at the display. Perhaps because Helene entered college rather young, she and my parents chose a women's junior college, William Woods, despite its unfortunate location in Missouri. That state, unlike Kansas, allowed the sale of liquor. Just as damnable, its Border Ruffians, in a pre–Civil War raid, had killed residents of Lawrence. Their graves lay near that of Dad's great-grandfather. A missionary to the Indians, Jonas Dodge had died in 1859 of pneumonia, but in family legend he survived as another early Lawrence martyr.

Free spirit though she was, Helene still had a strong sense of family obligation. I remember nothing but love and gentle instruction from her. Placed in charge of her baby brother, she recalled years later, she would read aloud from her current favorite, Thomas Wolfe's *Look Homeward, Angel*, while I gurgled with delight at the flow of his luxurious sentences.

Helene had me memorize Emily Dickinson's "I'm Nobody, Who are You?" and when, out on our sidewalk, I recited it for Lela, I learned something of the satisfaction of verbal performance. The morning that Helene pointed out how much better it would have been to put on both shoes rather than running downstairs twice to have them tied one at a time, she instilled in me the family respect for efficiency.

But with Ruth and Rena it must have been different.

Later Ruth told me how easy it would have been to despair with so talented and forceful an older sister.

When my mother's sister Verna died of cancer just before Christmas in 1936, we were far away across the state in Goodland. But the telephoned news (long-distance calls then were almost solely about a death) left my mother weeping quietly and wondering whether or not she could get back for the funeral. Ruth, a high school sophomore, had a date for that night. She insisted she should and would go. Told she must not, she shed tears of her own, angry ones. The decision was firm, and Helene felt obliged to help her accept it.

"Try to imagine how you would feel if this were Rena or Hughie."

My memory is vivid here, partly because of the tears, partly because of the parent-child conflict, but doubtless also because of the utterly new mention of my own possible death.

With Rena, thin-skinned and sometimes obstreperous, Helene could be more directive. Once when Rena persisted in using a forbidden phrase (something as egregious as "darn it"), Helene threatened to wash out her mouth with soap. Sometimes Rena would shout at whoever her tormentor happened to be, "Leave me alone!" The verbally gifted oldest sister then composed a monitory quatrain to chide and offer instruction:

> Leave-me-'lone Rena was quite a strange girl,
> Much like the young lady who had the famed curl.
> When she was good she was very, very good,
> But when she was bad she was horrid.

To hear this recited in the presence of Little Brother must have been hard to bear. Little Brother, for his part, was delighted. More than once I chanted those verses when I felt Rena was getting the better of me.

Although I thought of her as one of the grown-ups, Helene too had her brushes with parental authority. After she had attended Washburn for a year, she was slated to become assistant director of the college's publicity bureau. She showed promise as a journalist, and the one faculty member there whom we all knew by name was her journalism professor. But my parents learned of an opening for a teacher at a rural one-room school near Goodland. This would be a paying job and allow Helene to earn some money to help with tuition.

In her recollection of the event, when we discussed it years later, she had agreed to accept the position and only the chance arrival of a college friend made her reconsider. He told her, "This is ridiculous. You are well on your way at Washburn and if you take this job, you'll end up marrying some farmer out here and scrub your life away." With new resolve, Helene told the folks that she would take a part-time job in Topeka and live frugally, but was determined to go back. They relented.

My remembered version is less complex. Helene answers the telephone. "They are offering me the job," she says unhappily. Joy from my parents. "But I'll lose my position at the college if I don't go back."

"Nonsense. They'll hold it for you for next year." Helene cites a similar case in which "they" had done no such thing and leaves the room in tears.

Some time later, after a husband-wife conference, a resigned Mother is saying, "All right then, you can go." And with no conditions set.

Why is this so memorable? The always-in-control Helene close to defeat? Tears from a young adult? Yes, those, but most of all, another parent-child conflict, a situation into which I could all too easily project myself.

Once on a train ride with Helene, when I was five or six, the crowd forced us into different rows. With Helene right behind me, I entered into a fervent conversation with the charming and attentive lady next to me. I told her about our cats and dogs. Finding her responsive, I then launched into the tale of my sister's brush with schoolteaching. "And she cried," I solemnly concluded.

At the end of the trip, as we paused on the station platform, Helene gently admonished me, "It is fine to talk about kitties and doggies with a stranger, but not about things that make someone in the family cry." Mere volubility, it seemed, was not good in itself, and one's words could reach more than their immediately intended audience. I vowed to do better, but later in life sometimes wished I had taken this lesson even more to heart.

Ruth: The Etiquette Expert

> There are two types of criticism, destructive and constructive.
> —Ruth

Ruth, middle child of the five, liked to point out the burdensomeness of that position. She voiced her fantasies of being adopted (which Rena and I also experienced at times) the most often. She was, in fact, physically the most distinctive, though none of the five closely resembled any other. With eyes brown like my mother's and hair dark brown, she was the only daughter identified as a "brunette." That term, with its whiff of exoticism, did not seem inferior to "blonde" to me.

Tallest of the sisters, Ruth had wonderfully straight posture, an indication not so much of self-confidence as of determination. Years later she explained to me that she had chosen to be resolute as a way to overcome the discouragement of comparing herself to the bright, all-around activist Helene. It said much about Ruth's chosen persona that she disparaged people whom she labeled the "'scuse me for livin'" type.

We were all heavily coached on proper behavior and giving the right appearance, but Ruth took this instruction most deeply to heart. When the term "lady" lost its aura in the 1970s, Ruth still clung to it. Mother had told her that it took three generations to make a lady and that in our family only Ruth's generation had a chance to reach that pinnacle.

Evidence of Ruth's concern about social rank surfaced when in 1939 she left Goodland for Colorado Women's College in Denver. We lived then in the Fowler house at 1212 Walnut Street. When the printed student list arrived, Ruth's address appeared as "1212 Walnut Place." Of course, almost all the other students lived on streets, and a few on avenues. We teased her gently when mail arrived using the phony address, but she offered no apologies.

All the siblings except for me showed musical talent, playing instruments in school bands and singing in school and church choirs, but Ruth had the greatest gift. With measured praise, Mother used to say that Ruth's voice was "melodious, but not strong." Yet in school and church alike, she stood out because of her singing. Among her solos at church, I recall "My Task" as particularly compelling. The family discussed its various admonitions, which included "to love someone more dearly every day" and "to help a wandering child to find his way." Ruth sang spontaneously around the house, and others in the family soon knew her favorites by heart.

Apart from Ruth's joy in the music, choral singing appealed as an acceptable form of socializing that let her get out of the house in the evenings. She belonged to the church choir, of course. But I remember more vividly her singing in high school groups, such as the chorus in *H.M.S. Pinafore*. The dress she wore for the Girls Glee Club required a major sewing operation at home. The gold taffeta and black trim represented the colors of Sherman

County Consolidated High School. To indulge the director's whim, each dress had five strips of black gimp sewn on around the bottom, standing for the clef lines. As if this were not demanding enough, the lines had to be the same distance from the floor for every girl in the front row. The shorter the girl, the more of her calf she displayed. I watched fascinated during the repeated measurings to get this right on Ruth's dress.

Selection as second soprano in the Girls Quartet was Ruth's greatest musical honor. At least two in this group I can still conjure up in memory, the taller, darker Relda Lou, one of the altos and Ruth's best friend, and another girl who "got into trouble," or as my mother usually put it, "made a fool of herself." The quartet traveled to inter-school contests with Mr. Rice, the director. A gaunt fellow with round spectacles and slicked-back hair, he was one of only two bachelors on the high school staff. When he provided the only chaperonage, my parents hesitated before allowing Ruth to go on the quartet's trips to other towns. Ruth did not help her cause by reporting that Mr. Rice wanted to "spend an hour on my lips."

Whatever her self-doubts, and perhaps because of them, Ruth counted among the popular girls in the high school. Even late in life she enjoyed recalling that the Sherman Sals, the pep club, elected her queen her freshman year. She went out frequently on dates and soon had a steady boyfriend, a darkly handsome fellow, a year older. The fact that H. D. Fisk went by his initials added to his seeming maturity. Since these were also my initials, I felt a special bond and considered calling myself "H. D." But as a ten-year-old my attraction went beyond that, verging on infatuation. During one of his evening visits, when he and Ruth hoped for some time alone in the living room, I pestered him until he got a rope from his car and tied me up, dumping me in one of the bedrooms. I never confessed my pleasure in this assault and did not support Mother's later surmise that my (mild) back problems traced to this "manhandling."

Whereas Helene brought excitement with her alternation of absences and gift-laden arrivals, Ruth provided daily company and steady guidance. Her manicuring paraphernalia, bought with her own money, intrigued me. Using her emery board, unique in the family, she smoothed her fingernails before applying nailpolish and sitting in splendid inactivity while they dried. I recall her consulting the family's little-used and surely out-of-date etiquette book. The author was not Emily Post, but rather the similarly named Emily Holt, who perhaps benefited from the resemblance of the names. Ruth read relevant passages aloud. One explained the art of the bread-and-butter letter, sent to a hostess after a visit, another, the niceties of introducing a man to a woman.

Some of Ruth's pointers were her own creations. To slow yourself down while eating, she suggested, put your hands in your lap from time to time and just chew. Sometimes her counsel came in response to my direct questions, such as, "What should you do if someone gives you a present you don't really like?" Answer: "Say thanks politely and then say as little as possible." One day, before telling me about something I had done wrong, she carefully explained the difference between "destructive" criticism and "constructive" criticism. I've forgotten the nature of my misdeed, but her guide to evaluating criticism stayed etched in my memory.

When Ruth brought home her first college yearbook, I devoured it, relishing the compliments to her that other students had inscribed beside their photographs. One proved unforgettable: "Always admired you for that special quality—'tact' Prof. Brandon called it."

Just the word, I thought. That was what made Ruth so special.

Rena: The Rival

You're the baby of the family, so of course you're
spoiled.

—Rena

A photograph in the family album showed me as a baby in
Dad's arms, with Rena looking resentfully up at us.
Youngest and next-to-youngest among the children, a five-
year age difference added to strains between us. She liked
to tease me about being spoiled. Looking back, I feel sure I
was indulged in ways she was not. Like most families of
that time, ours granted more freedom to boys than to girls.
As the last child, I provided the final chance to apply lessons of childrearing learned during my parents' married
life. They had gradually moderated their standards of dis-
cipline, and besides, I was innately a gentler person, an
observer and commenter. Rambunctious Rena laughed
hard, cried hard, and felt herself embattled. I remember
episodes of what was called "flouncing from the room."

Schoolwork did not come particularly easily for Rena,
as it would for me. I took pride in my report cards, but the
folks paid disappointingly little attention to my good
grades, perhaps to avoid invidious comparisons. Patiently,
with book propped up above the dishpan, Mother would
help Rena with spelling lessons as they did the dishes and I
stood by envying their collaboration.

In retrospect it is easy to recognize the discomfort of
Rena's position. I conclude that being named after our
mother was as much an irritant for her as an honor, especially since the aunts persisted in calling her "Little Rena."
As the third daughter, she found herself placed between a
younger brother and two older sisters, one a model student
and social sophisticate, the other a gifted vocalist, popular
among fellow high schoolers. Rena could vent frustrations

Whatever the issue between Mother and Rena, I am staying out of it. Author's collection.

on the younger brother, but she could also make him her ally. We became both competitors and comrades.

She took satisfaction in belittling her rival. At about age nine, already indulging in recollection, I asked her, "Do you remember the time I put milk on my grapefruit?"

"Oh, yes. That was when we all began to realize that there was something a little off about you."

Not quite the jolly reminiscence I was seeking.

In a much later effort to have Rena share memories (we were both in our seventies), I pursued a suspicion aroused by having found repeated references in old family correspondence to Hughie's (the baby's) coming down with a cold and by recollecting that my worried parents had had my tonsils removed when I was two years old. Then too, there had been the evening dose of cod liver oil, the molasses-flavored Myledol.

"Rena," I asked in a chatty long-distance phone conversation, "was I a sickly child?"

The answer came promptly. This was not a new issue with her. "No, but you were treated as if you were. That's why I had to be so hard on you."

Reassured, and better understanding our ambivalent childhood bond, I found myself recalling some of the ways I had defended myself.

When I was a second grader, Rena and I attended the same Goodland elementary school and both came home at noon for lunch. During this break from school, Rena would read the morning paper's comics to me. A crisis came when she refused to keep reading *Jane Arden* aloud. "It's turning into a love story, and you're too young to hear that."

Resenting this bar to grown-up knowledge, I began secretly to read *Jane Arden* for myself, and soon all the other comics as well. Alas, the encounters of Jane and her male admirer revealed nothing I had not already observed elsewhere, and Rena gave me no credit when I announced my independence. "Good. It was boring to have to read to you anyway."

Rena had one of those bright, morning faces. I think of her forehead and nose as always shiny, maybe a little too shiny. Her posture, her smile, her hairdo, observed now in early family snapshots, display much of the charm audiences found in girl-next-door actresses like Judy Garland. I lived not next door, but under the same roof, and this charm largely escaped me.

Instead of admiring her looks, I teased Rena by calling her fat. Perhaps it began in revenge for her calling me spoiled, perhaps it was just little-brother deviltry. At least once the taunt brought her to tears. Mother assured us both that Rena was just "pleasingly plump." I doubt if the phrase brought Rena much consolation. To tell the truth, I never thought of her as fat. It was just the available insult.

But what was it that escalated insult to physical attack? Something she wouldn't give me? Something she said? All I recall is seizing a newly sharpened pencil and jabbing her twice in the upper arm. In this case Mother did not take the middle ground. Her rebuke brought shame, if not quite remorse. "Hughie, Rena will have these marks for the rest of her life."

She calmed Rena's sobs and washed the spots with Zonite, then the family's standard disinfectant. I had in fact tattooed my sister. Years later she would show these small black dots to her children, warning them of the lasting results of violence.

As comrade, Rena was my model and my helper. She could explain some of the mysteries of the school and the neighborhood. In Herington, she had made sure I looked both ways before crossing the street, and I listened with sympathy as she told of the meanness of a wicked classmate named Betsy Carpenter. After our move to Goodland, I admired her steady correspondence with Elizabeth Tripp back in Herington, envying her the letters that arrived with her name on the envelope.

Gradually, and well before we left Goodland, the positive side of our relationship gained dominance. Just being the two youngest, the "not old enough to" siblings, often made us natural allies. Trapped in the back seat of the car while an older family member pursued some endless errand downtown, we could amuse ourselves with games like "My father owns a grocery store." This let us conjure up the products in the store and stretch our minds to find ones that began with unlikely letters of the alphabet.

"And in that store there is a 'k.'"

That was a hard one, but an acceptable answer came to mind. "Kale! My turn now."

Not the most exciting game, but better than twiddling our thumbs, the family code name for boring inactivity.

Once, for a week or so, Rena was responsible for getting my lunch, Mother having gone to Topeka, probably to help Helene select her trousseau. Although Rena was enrolled in home economics, a subject in which she thrived, the cooking part of the course had just begun. "The only thing I've learned how to make is milkshakes. Would that be OK?"

Would it ever!

"What shall we mix in today—banana, peach, or prune?" We tried them one by one, each seeming better than the last. A new bond grew, a shared guilty indulgence that violated the doctrine of the well-balanced diet.

Rena did well in high school in Goodland and became a happier person. More and more I valued her comradeship and took pride in the triumphs she reported. Though never a soloist like Ruth, she sang in the glee club. She had dates with Darle Fortmeyer, who lived on the farm his grandparents had homesteaded. His face was as scrubbed and shiny as Rena's, and when he called at the house he showed "perfect manners."

Her geometry report brought great success. On its stiff blue cover, she had inked a geometrized owl. The paper came back with an A and Mr. Engel's comment, "Nice work. White ink hard to handle." I was nearly as jubilant as she, jubilant enough to recall the exact words all these years later.

Electing more home economics than required, Rena soon passed beyond the limit of milkshakes. During her last year in Goodland she enrolled in a newly offered course, Girls' Shop, a leap across gender barriers that impressed me with its daring. Dad bought the walnut boards for the dressing table she planned, boasting a double-curved front and shelves at each end, a difficult "modernistic" design she had found in a magazine.

Our move from Goodland in 1940, forced by another Rock Island consolidation, hit Rena hard. Halfway though high school and president-elect of the Future Homemakers of America, she had to leave a close circle of friends as well as teachers who knew and respected her. Adjusting to a larger high school full of strangers was to prove difficult.

These forced relocations among railroad towns affected all five siblings. But another sort of movement added tension. Much as we wanted to be respected in the present, among neighbors and in school and church, we hoped to gain status in some future, wider setting. Our parents nourished such hopes, helping us see a world beyond the town.

CHAPTER 3

Grade School

We don't talk in class without raising our hand.

—Miss Zarnowski

WATCHING other children pass our house in Herington on their way to Lincoln School, I had felt left out, even as a four-year-old. Like thousands of others I asked, "When can I go to school?" The answer, "When you're a little older," was memorably frustrating. After an eon of waiting, I turned six, and on that very day school opened and I headed for the first grade.

Rena advised me to pick a seat in the front row. Not quite sure what that meant, I chose a seat in the first file of desks along the wall, second from the front. The smiling boy in front of me turned to carry on our conversation, begun while waiting in line. Miss Zarnowski made an example of us, pointing out gently that we shouldn't talk in class. But by no means did she mark me as a troublemaker. With this offense soon obliterated by good behavior, I was moved to the back of the room with the explanation, "I know I don't have to keep an eye on you."

It was exciting to know kids from other neighborhoods. Some of them had problems new to me. When the class celebrated Halloween, Mary Louise received an apple, not candy like the rest of us. She smiled as if she liked being special, but we knew she had "sugar-di-beetis." When Miss

Zarnowski asked us to bring items of canned goods for the food drive, Joey raised his hand and announced, "I can't. We need to get some of that ourselves." Nobody on South C Street would have needed to say that.

My intense fondness for Miss Zarnowski in Herington set a pattern. My feelings were just as enthusiastically positive for my teachers in grades two through five, in Goodland. Of some I have a photograph. Even without that reminder, however, they come to mind clearly, their individuality not blurred by the affection that sheathed them all.

At the new WPA-built Grant School, close to the Kimmel house, our second rented home in Goodland, Miss Cessna kept the second grade lively. She often left her desk, moving about the classroom with the grace of a dancer. For spelling period each day she had us shift from our regular seats and take places according to how we were doing, in a continuing contest. One child could displace another by correctly spelling a word that had been "missed" by the one immediately ahead. A good speller and an eager competitor, I gradually moved from the last desk to the first, and just then the game ended, without any fanfare or prize. I didn't need a prize. Moving forward had given steady joy along the way.

In arithmetic too I thrived. For me every number had a gender and age, as with the fat lady 8 and the dapper gentleman 7. Personalizing the digits, which involved quarrels, marriages, and progeny, may have slowed my calculations, but it brought adventure to adding, subtracting, and multiplying. Health habits, then required by Kansas law (probably because of lobbying by the Women's Christian Temperance Union), caught my interest in a different way, partly through the warning illustrations in the assigned book. This subject lacked the precision of spelling and arithmetic, and the tests—consisting of questions such as "Did you

wash your hands every time after going to the toilet?"—
were never graded. Still, I began rigorously washing my
hands in order to give the right answer.

The classroom offered one satisfaction after another, but
recess on the grassless playground altered relationships.
Twice I got into trouble out there.

My first victim was Rosa, an exotic beauty whose black
curls shook when she laughed. I found her fascinating.
Whether as part of a game or an effort to steal a kiss, I can't
remember, but I grabbed at her waist that day as she pulled
away. Her black dress tore along one side, exposing her
white underwear. She began to sob, then ran back into the
classroom. Miss Cessna rose to the challenge. She told
Rosa not to cry and magically produced needle and thread
to match the damaged fabric. "It was just an accident," I
explained. The incident was closed before the rest of the
class came in from the playground.

My second turn to violence stirred deeper fears. Albert,
the classmate I assaulted, was nobody's pal. One of his
shoes lacked shoestrings, and his overalls grew greasier
week by week. Perhaps our quarrel broke out over whose
turn came next, perhaps over rightful possession of some
small found object. After an exchange of insults, I punched
him hard. I remember no tears in this case, but something
worse, Albert surrounded by supporters who announced,
"We're going to tell."

Facing disaster and imagining that Miss Cessna would
send me to the principal's office, I headed for home. After a
few minutes of unconvincing excuses for my premature
return, my parents extracted the truth. My father, who was
home on his weekly "day off," assured me that he would
go back with me and that returning that very day was
important. Dad and Miss Cessna consulted in the hall.
Then I returned sheepishly to my seat, believing that I
hadn't a friend in the class. The spelling champion, perhaps

the teacher's pet, had been disgraced. The other students seemed to have forgotten the episode by the next day, but for me it was engraved for life.

After Mrs. Kimmel's return to Goodland in mid-1937 required us to move—to the Fowler house across town—I changed schools. Though a long walk away, the nearest school was Central, an older two-story building with worn cement steps and respectable trees in its playground. Our third grade teacher, Miss Olsen, whose classroom was on the first floor, began by sharing a little joke with us. Some students, it seemed, were so naïve as to think that moving upstairs to grades five through eight meant going to high school. Laughing together at that made us all feel good.

Miss Olsen was pretty in a different way from Miss Cessna, with marcelled hair and heavy lipstick. The lips were almost always smiling. We applied a word from the movie ads to her: she was "glamorous."

Mr. Gibson, the band director, who came by the school occasionally to give individual instrument lessons, had the habit of dropping into our classroom about once a week and chatting in a corner with Miss Olsen. To judge by her vivacity, the visits provided an attractive respite from pedagogy. We students welcomed these brief interruptions and admired the tableau. But one day while Mr. Gibson was still in the room, Patrick unwisely raised his hand and announced, "There's going to be a wedding."

"Who . . . ?" asked the flabbergasted music man.

"Why, you two, of course."

Miss Olsen stayed calm. "Nice thought," she declared, with a theatrical smile toward her visitor, who coughed and departed.

Then the smile disappeared. "That wasn't funny, Patrick. All these other teachers here and Mr. Johnson the janitor are my friends, and that's all."

I assume I was not the only one terrified by the change in

our gentle teacher. That afternoon we all remained very quiet. The next day Miss Olsen's classroom smile was back, but we never had another visit from Mr. Gibson.

It was she who gave me the D in art, but I didn't much hold that against her. After all, I did tend to color outside the lines. Though that grade still rankles a bit, it is over-shadowed by a remembered triumph in her class. The assignment was to find flowers beginning with all the let-ters of the alphabet. Nobody could come up with an *x*. In back of the Fowler house, luckily for me, a young florist operated a small commercial greenhouse. Emboldened to go to an expert, I entered his steamy domain and made my inquiry. Nothing came to mind, he said, but he could check in the big catalogue he kept on hand. Sure enough, there in the close-printed pages stood the name of an unpronounce-able *x* flower. The lack of a picture bothered me not at all. I copied off the multisyllabic name and learned that arcane knowledge lies stored in books.

Required to keep thirty restless eight-year-olds occupied, Miss Olsen instituted the practice of letting those who had finished the arithmetic assignment help others still working at it, joining them in their seats. I would breeze through the problems and, sometimes first of all, signal my readiness to help out. Why were these episodes remembered? Below the satisfaction of playing teacher pulsed the visceral pleasure of changing seats, snuggling close to another student, and murmuring suggestions—all with Miss Olsen's permission.

Much older than Miss Olsen, the fourth-grade teacher, Miss Duell, portrayed for us a benign grandmother. Gray-ing hair and lack of makeup made us think of her as much older than her probable fifty-five years. She was not given to continuous smiling, but something about her manner gave steady reassurance. "Since my name is Duell," she told us the first day, "some folks think I like to fight. But that's wrong, the opposite of the truth."

Miss Grace Duell and her fourth graders. I am in the next to top row, left end. Author's collection.

She and her sister, both unmarried, lived in a small neat frame house across the street from Central School. I hadn't known where any of my other teachers lived. They had simply appeared each day from nowhere. It was easier to think of Miss Duell as flesh and blood.

The other teachers had tolerated Harold, an oversized boy with a grin so wide that he drooled. He was not disruptive, just a hopeless case. We could all see that he was too dumb to count. Miss Duell sat him a little apart from the rest of the class and between our lessons gave him elementary reading and arithmetic instruction. Although we had no desire to take parallel measures by letting Harold into our games, we did discuss her action among ourselves and praised her generosity.

I experienced Miss Duell's indulgence in an incident made memorable by shame. The class was building a model house and had reached the stage of interior decoration. We needed some sheer curtain fabric for the tiny windows. Miss Duell thought she had some at home, but I eagerly volunteered that we had some at our house. (I had wondered, in fact, why my mother was saving it.) I promised to bring it the next day.

How comforting to recall that nine-year-olds, not just septuagenarians, have things slip their minds. When the moment came to produce the fabric, I had to confess my forgetfulness. Miss Duell said, "My sister told me I should bring some in case the student didn't come through, but I told her, 'No, I don't have to worry about this one.'" This chance to see myself as someone in authority saw me only deepened my self-reproach, which no doubt showed in my face. "Don't worry. I won't tell her any different," she assured me.

Apparently the ability to retain episodic memories increases gradually as a child ages. In any case, I remember more about the fifth grade, when I was ten, than any of the earlier ones. Here the teacher was Miss Woodring, less alluring than Miss Olsen, bespectacled, but no grandmother, perhaps a trusted aunt. If she sent someone to stand in the hall, for whispering or chewing gum, even the miscreant called her judgment fair. We responded enthusiastically to each day's agenda and took pride in memorizing the capitals of all the states and territories, though I felt somewhat cheated after Dean told me that in his day students learned both each state's capital and its largest city.

Especially popular was Miss Woodring's reading aloud to us in the first period after lunch, a custom that no doubt aided digestion and allowed for surreptitious naps. Never tempted to nap, I was always disappointed at how quickly she announced, "End of chapter. That's all for today." The selected books had either children or animals as protagonists. *Greyfriars Bobby*, grim but still fascinating, told of a dog faithful to its master's grave.

Sometimes she would insert a bit of personal interpretation and sometimes disagree with an author's aside. A chapter in one book concluded with the assertion that the young hero "had yet to learn that when adults make a mistake, the last thing they will do is tell a child." Miss Woodring was slightly incensed. "Why, if I made a mistake, the first one I'd tell would be a child." We had no doubt she was on our side.

These readings were all the more welcome because that year the state board had discarded the beloved Bobbs-Merrill readers with their captivating illustrations and classic tales and poems that our parents could often recall. The substitute series included extracts from very recent publications, unsatisfactory snippets too realistic to let the imagination run free and not helped by slightly muddy photographs. Nothing of the contents remains in memory, only the repellent form.

Some teachers are shocked to find out that it is not the subject matter but rather the throw-away personal anecdote that former students recall years later. Out of all our hours together, it is one of Miss Woodring's casual reminiscences that comes back most distinctly.

"Yes, my name is the same as Governor Woodring's. When he came to town during his first campaign, I actually met him down in front of the Hotel Goodland. I walked right up to him and said, 'My name is Woodring too. Could we be related?' He said, 'Well, I certainly wouldn't mind being related to a nice young woman like you.'" Then she interpreted the incident: "Soft-soaped me and got my vote!"

Memorable—why? The precisely located scene with dialogue? The connection to someone of prominence? The warning about how politicians behave? More than any of these, I suspect it is because of the self-mockery in "Soft-soaped me and got my vote!"

Did I learn more from the teachers or the students? I was more certain of my acceptance by the teachers. Miss Olsen even confided that she did not call on me when my hand was up because she knew I could answer and wanted to give others a chance.

Though not always as positive, the influence of other children struck just as deeply. On the playground a rigid hierarchy of grade level held, but elsewhere the bounds were looser. Sometimes I got to know my friends' older or younger siblings, whom I often found just as much fun, but Phyllis's big brother brought big trouble.

Just why, in my first year at Central School, Phyllis drew my affection now seems inexplicable. Perhaps the freckles that peppered her nose and cheeks intrigued me. Her family lived a few blocks away from mine, and I passed her house regularly. One day, when a mattress was propped up in her yard, another boy told me that her grandmother had just died and they were airing the bedding. My sympathy for Phyllis swelled. Shortly thereafter, as we walked a little apart from the others heading home from school, I told her that I loved her.

Her brother Pete, two years older, interpreted this avowal as an affront to family honor, or at least as an excuse to pose as defender of his sister. Accompanied by two other boys from his grade, he accosted me one afternoon as I walked home alone. "Did you say you loved my sister?" I sheepishly admitted it. His eyes narrowed, his fists balled, and after a few menacing words, he battered my chest and shoulders.

This bullying, which soon seemed to be its own justification, continued for three days. Ashamed of the whole matter, I never considered telling my parents. But Mother had a habit of looking her children up and down. She discerned a bruised eye and asked hard questions. Mortified, I explained the source. I thought of it as my fault. I had indeed made the alleged advance to Pete's sister.

Matters were taken in hand. The next morning Dad came to the school. Miss Olsen asked me to step out into the hall with her. We assembled with Dad, Pete, and his classroom teacher in the privacy of "the boys' basement." (This euphemism survived even when, as in this case, the toilets were on the first floor.) The stink of urine and the oddity of seeing adults in this room intensified the memory. I also remember my inner sense of phoniness when I defended my remark to Phyllis. "The Bible says we are supposed to love everybody." Pete was not punished, simply warned. He left me alone, and I carefully crossed the street if I saw him ahead.

I thought it a point in my favor that I hadn't hit back. But Dad took the occasion to instruct me that a blow just below the ribs would sicken an opponent without doing permanent damage. I felt instinctively that this response wouldn't work for me. Doubtless in the tough environs of Badger Crick and the railroad tracks, it had been an effective tactic. Or even closer to home. Many years later my father confided that his older brother had tyrannized over him until the victim beat the tar out of his tormentor.

During recess, outdoors, segregated by grade and sex, I was happiest when the exchange was one to one. Gene Lee Beem, a spunky redhead, breezy and full of jokes, inspired a bit of awe because of the two stumps on his right hand. He told us how he had lost the fingers, though I've forgotten the story now. What I recall is a moment of intimacy while we talked under one of the Chinese elms that edged the playground. Suddenly he held out the damaged hand and urged, "Touch them." With a mixture of dread, curiosity, and desire to please, I rubbed my fingers against the stubs. The ends were not quite smooth, distorted by little ridges where the skin had been sewn together. I swallowed hard but was careful not to pull my hand away too quickly. He seemed satisfied. We had always gotten along.

My biggest frustrations came with the intrusion of team games. I enjoyed the challenges of red rover, although I rarely broke the other line, and sometimes failed to stop someone's break into ours. Softball was the heartache.

Only in the fifth grade did that cursed game get started, with its complicated rules and clear distinctions of individual skill. Maybe some of the boys asked Miss Woodring to organize it. In any case, there we were in the classroom one day with the two best sportsmen, Donald Scott and Bob Parker, named captains and all the other boys told to stand. We were then picked for the two teams alternately, with the two captains showing astute perception of talent. As I had foreseen, I was the last chosen. I bore it. I couldn't consider the judgment any less than fair.

On the paced-out baseball diamond in the bare center of the playground, the captain relegated me to right outfield, where happily the ball almost never came. It surprised me later to hear that great hitters are frequently assigned that position. I was anything but. Though there was nothing tricky about the pitching, I rarely got wood on the ball, and when I did, couldn't make it to first base. Mostly I struck out.

For some reason we repeated the selection process after a month, forming new teams. This time there turned out to be an odd number of candidates, and I was left standing at the end. Miss Woodring declared me umpire. This relieved me of the pressure to play, but it subjected me to shouts of derision as I gave my best estimate of balls, strikes, and tags. Donald Scott showed particular outrage and by sheer willpower sometimes overruled my calls.

"Out? He was safe by a mile! You must need glasses."

Given these blows to my ego, imagine my excitement

when Miss Woodring chose me for a crossing guard. Well, not exactly. The crossing guards, who wore silver badges and broad white elastic belts and had permission to arrive a little late and leave early, had long since been chosen. Donald Scott and Bob Parker, of course, as well as Tommy Barrett. But when Tommy began to take trumpet lessons that kept him from his morning stint on Tuesdays and Thursdays, I was chosen to fill in. The guard's duty was not to stop cars but merely to signal students when it was safe to cross Main Street to the schoolyard.

The announcement of my triumph brought little support at home. Mother responded with a sinister explanation: the coming of winter weather had made someone drop the duty. Stubbornly insisting that I had already accepted, I tried to convey the honor involved. Mother grudgingly assented, but sent me downtown with Dad to buy a pair of galoshes, ghastly floppy things with impossible buckles. I was allowed to perform the new duty, but the bulging galoshes detracted considerably from the splendor of the badge and belt.

After fifth-grade classes ended in the spring, feeling a little lonesome for the old schoolyard, Gene Lee and I went there to play. The empty grounds gave us a chance to explore corners never assigned as play areas. We climbed on top of the cement incinerator, a previously overlooked structure, and peered inside. Much to our surprise, there lay Miss Woodring's grade books, still unburned. We fished them out, though Gene Lee showed little interest. Guiltily aware of the invasion of privacy, I inspected the inner pages. There in neat rows and columns stood all our names and regular grade entries, one subject on each page. Then, in the final column, the grade for the year.

I was fascinated by the orderliness, the statistical precision, and, no doubt, by the evident power to judge. It must be wonderfully satisfying to be a teacher. Years later, when

I began teaching at Chapel Hill, I kept similar grade books. The initial pleasure didn't last. I shifted to amassing sheets of scrawled names and grades in manila folders, tossing away the spiral grade books that the department secretary persisted in distributing.

CHAPTER 4

The Christian Church

All lovers of Christ welcome.

—Church mimeographed program, under "Communion"

AFTER the school year ended, the school board turned Central over to the local churches for a week of Daily Vacation Bible School. Students came from all the Protestant churches in town. I found the new faces appealing, and best of all, we were placed according to the grade we would enter in the fall. Having finished the fourth grade, my first experience with Vacation Bible School took place upstairs in the fifth-grade classroom, in June, a forecast of maturity.

The cheerful amateur teachers believed in hands-on learning. We created a movie theater in a shoebox, where our colored drawings, pasted on a long roll of paper, could be rolled past the opening by two hand-manipulated wooden axles. Our independent film, based on an account the teachers had presented earlier, told of a stricken city's reaction to a disastrous flood. The Red Cross and other charities appeared in leading roles, but my only sharp memory of the story reflects the teachers' horrifying explanation of "looters." Their wickedness had required National Guard patrols.

Perhaps because of the interdenominationalism, God-talk was minimized. God ranked as one character in selected Bible stories.

These June classes were special. Most of my religious activities occurred in the white clapboard Christian Church, located about halfway between the Fowler house and downtown. This denomination, strong in the Midwest, had been chosen by Grandmother Eddy when she moved into Topeka and left her rural community church behind. My parents entered her church when they set up housekeeping in Topeka, staying with the denomination when they moved first to Herington, then to Goodland.

In the welter of denominational names, the "Christian Church" brought considerable confusion. I knew we belonged to the Christian Church, but sometimes when I announced this, I met the objection, "Which one? All churches are Christian." Complicating the matter, Mother advised us never to let anyone confuse ours with the "Church of Christ," a smaller, radically evangelical denomination. Only years later did I hear the formal national name "Disciples of Christ."

The fabled bitter rivalry between Baptists and Methodists provided material for jokes in our family. Although we heard aspersions on the Baptists' "closed communion" and criticism of the Methodists' frequent relocation of pastors, we didn't dwell on such distinctions. Nor did we set great store by denominational loyalty. Grandmother Eddy had been reared a Baptist, Grandmother Hawkins a Methodist. One family friend confided that when she married, her husband shifted to her church and she to his political party. That struck us as sensible.

When Grandmother Hawkins and Aunt Kit visited, we took greater care about grace before meals. They had long been staunch Free Methodists, a church Dad had abandoned in boyhood. Phrases from hymns, theological classics, and the Bible sprinkled their conversation. Grandmother Hawkins claimed to have read through the Bible four times, but the pace at which she turned the pages raised doubts in my mind.

She spent hours working on squares cut from fabric remnants to make gathered rosettes for a new quilt. When one day I asked her why she wasn't working on her quilt, she pointed out the obvious. "Because today is Sunday, of course." I realized I had betrayed our family's laxity. Sensing my dismay, she comforted me. "Now, you just forgot, didn't you?"

Although I had heard about Roman Catholics, out of whose mysterious legions came candidates who ran against my uncles and benefited from endorsements by their priests, the intense opposition of Grandmother Hawkins, usually so gentle, bewildered me. Coming across a magazine photograph of the coronation ceremony for Pius XII, she scoffed, "Look at all those priests crawling up to kiss the Pope's toe!" When Aunt Kit conveyed the surprising news that Cousin Beulah, still unmarried in middle age, had now found a husband, she quickly added, "But we hear he's a Roman Catholic." Clearly, continued spinsterhood would have been preferable to such a match.

My experiences in our safely Protestant church divided sharply between the Sunday-school basement and the more imposing, walnut-pewed sanctuary upstairs. My first encounter with Sunday school in Goodland, when we lived in the Cherry Street house, had not gone well. Rena led me past the "Cradle Roll" to the room for the Primary, those aged four to six, and left me on my own. Although not given to whispering, I did respond to overtures. When the little boy next to me asked how much I had brought for the collection, I confided that I had three pennies. He had an astonishing nickel.

Further arousal of envy and emulation came a few minutes later. After we heard the story of the Good Samaritan,

Goodland's First Christian Church. Its baptistery was a tank under the stage. Courtesy of Parker Collection, Sherman County Historical Society.

the teacher posed a moral challenge. "What would you do if you had an apple and you met a little boy who was hungry but didn't have one?" I suspected the answer was "Give him the apple," but I hesitated to speak out. A slightly older girl in the front row self-confidently announced that she would take the apple home, have her mother cut it in half, and so share it with the hungry child. I knew this had to be the right solution because our leader glowed, called in another teacher, and had the young know-it-all repeat her answer.

Things went better for me in Intermediate. Each Sunday, by reciting a memorized Bible verse, you gained a new gold star next to your name on the wall chart. Never failing in either attendance or recitation, I soon found stars being glued on top of other stars. Although the teacher never made comparisons, it was clear to me, and I assumed to everybody, that I had the most.

With or without stars by our names, we were all promoted each year. As fifth graders we found that we had the youngest Sunday school teacher yet. This was Miss Griest, about my sister Ruth's age and much admired for her clarinet solos at evening church services. Her family ran the best auto repair shop in town. The slogan over its door struck me as immensely clever: "You wreck 'em. We fix 'em." Thin almost to the point of boniness and wearing stylish rimless glasses, Miss Griest kept the class interested, moving from a little talk about a biblical passage to a bit of moral-pointing discussion. We all liked her from the first, but she gained heroic stature when she arranged a theater party for us.

On the agreed evening we gathered in front of the local cinema. Miss Griest paid for our tickets, a dime each, not a nickel as at matinees, and we sat down to watch the not-altogether-clear romantic imbroglios of *Winter Carnival*. Best of all, she had brought candy bars. These were handed down the row and consumed even before the short subjects ended.

Later I was telling someone—another stranger on a train?—that I had two wonderful teachers that year and that although promotion would end my connection with Miss Woodring, Miss Griest would stay in my life as Faye because she had married my brother. Yes, such was the case. My misogynist brother had found love. In fact, Dean accompanied the class on the epochal theater party.

After Sunday school some youngsters went home, but I joined others in my family upstairs for the main service. The challenge was to sit quietly as Reverend Ratner conducted the service. Knowing when to bow one's head and joining in the Lord's Prayer (in our church we used the more sibilant "trespasses," not "debts") somewhat relieved the tedium. After the sermon the last hymn served as an "invitation" to "declare Jesus the Christ the son of the living God and your personal savior." This moment brought delightful suspense, but it was a rare Sunday when anyone came forward.

The preacher's sermons allowed time for daydreaming or shoving back the cuticle on my fingernails, as I had observed Ruth do during her self-manicures. The content of the sermons escaped me, but the ability to sit patiently while an authority spoke served me well later on.

Hoping to increase attendance, the minister announced the topic of a forthcoming evening sermon two weeks in advance: "What is the Unforgivable Sin?" He encouraged members to drop their written answers into a box in the vestibule. At home my mother gave us her conjecture. The unforgivable sin occurs when you don't stop after a sin but just keep on sinning. That sounded reasonable, and meant a lot more to me than the minister's recondite answer: "the sin against the Holy Ghost."

Of course we respected the Ten Commandments, but the Bible counted as only one among various bases for moral wisdom. Mother's suggestion that people make their own hell right here on earth was hardly scriptural, but she did occasionally rely on the Bible as her authority, memorably in the warning, "Whoever calls his brother a fool is in danger of hellfire." I never heard at home that the devil can quote scripture, but a similar skepticism underlay one of our standard anecdotes. When rebuked at the dinner table for being a greedy boy, Uncle Jess had defended himself with the brash claim, "The Bible says to always take the biggest potato on the plate."

The Christian Church observed communion every Sunday morning, not quarterly, as with the Methodists. The symbols of Christ's body and blood comprised wafers on a silver tray and wine, really grape juice, in about twenty tiny glasses set in the round openings of another salver. These were both passed from hand to hand in the pews, and the mimeographed program declared, "All lovers of Christ welcome." Our Sunday school teachers explained the contrast with "closed communion," the less tolerant, members-only practice in other denominations.

Whereas the adults solemnly partook, I was judged too young. This, even after I had whispered, "But, Mother, I'm already five." Worse yet, Rena had been baptized and took the "bread and wine" with scornful superiority, reaching across me to hand the tray to the next insider.

Eager to end this exclusion, I paid careful attention to the special Sunday school training that readied us to "make our confession of faith." One glorious morning during the invitation hymn, a few of us eight-year-olds shyly walked down the aisle and answered yes to the minister's formulaic question about our belief. Later, Ruth had to correct me when I referred to this as "swearing us in." For some reason the next step was delayed, and I was the last of my group to be baptized.

Though trying to be tolerant of the "sprinkling" or "pouring" in other denominations, the Christian Church practiced "total immersion," reasoning from the biblical language describing Jesus' baptism. For its baptistery the Goodland church relied on a large tank under the stage. One Sunday evening a few weeks after my confession of faith, with the covering boards removed and my family among the congregation, Reverend Ratner led me down the steps into the water and baptized me "in the name of the Father, the Son, and the Holy Ghost." In the changing room he had carefully instructed me to take a deep breath and hold it. I came through the ceremony without choking, slipping, or other mishap. The male togetherness afterward, as the preacher and I dried ourselves and changed clothes, put a special seal on the occasion.

One other person was baptized that night, but she was a young woman, who of course changed in a different room.

Soon after my baptism, in 1938, a big weeklong revival took place in a vacant hall on Main Street. Our minister, along with the other Protestant clergymen in town, had invited the evangelist. Each night those who came forward at the concluding invitation were asked to name a local church in which to share their newly declared faith. Among those who were already church members, some walked to the front to rededicate themselves to Christ. Emotions unstirred in ordinary Sunday services were roused by the oratorical energy of the evangelist, the size of the audience, and the compelling pulse of hymns like "Beulah Land" and "Bringing in the Sheaves."

Although no Billy Sunday, the revivalist proved strong medicine for troubled souls in Goodland. During each sermon he would rip off his coat and loosen his necktie as he worked up a good sweat. Doubtless he spoke of God and Jesus, but none of the theology has stayed with me. I conjecture that he focused on the seven deadly sins, one per night.

I do recall his tale of a young man who died from cigarette smoking. Toward the end, the emaciated fellow had grown so weak that his father had to slip the cigarette between his lips and light it for him. After this cautionary tale, it was quite superfluous to have someone say in the car on our way home, "You wouldn't ever smoke, would you, Hughie?"

The evangelist's son, an athletic fellow with an easy smile, took charge of the youth, leading special sessions for us in the afternoons and on Saturday. Though the group was large, he kept us happy and attentive. We learned some new hymns, and we learned, by singing them, all the books of the Old and New Testaments in proper order. He knew just how many to introduce each day. If the tune seemed somewhat forced and chantlike, the rhythmical sequence of "Genesis, Exodus, Leviticus, Numbers . . ." was embedded in us for years to come, as well as the triumphal conclusion: "Jude and Revelation!" On the final night of the revival we gathered onstage to show off our musical memorization before the biggest audience of the week.

Because of the son, I remember another bit of the evangelist's sermons. His theme this time was the sin of sloth, and he declared that laziness infected his own family. Turning toward his son, who sat onstage during the services, he announced, "And the laziest of the lot is close enough to spit on." Recognizing an undeserved insult to my new idol, I felt vindicated when Mother declared the comment "in bad taste."

Family standards must not yield, even before the Lord's anointed.

CHAPTER 5

My Mother and My Father

The older children have always helped in rearing the
younger ones.

—My mother

Not one of her daughters can match her ankles.

—My father

M Y MOTHER graduated from Washburn Academy, a
matter of some pride among her children, which
reflected her own. Had she gone to college? No, but,
she explained, "If I had tutored that summer, I could
have entered Washburn College as a sophomore."
Instead she had married—at age eighteen, much too young,
she assured her daughters.

Although of no interest to me during my childhood, her
graduation and wedding photographs showed Mother to
have been a great beauty, with dark hair and eyes, clear
complexion, and a look of serene willingness to be photographed. My father had caught his first glimpse of her as
she came downstairs in her home at Indian Hill Farm. He
was boarding there, having recently taken a job nearby as a
Rock Island operator. I more than once heard him comment on the loveliness of her ankles, first observed on this

My parents on their wedding day, 1910. Mother explained that brides stood in order to display their gowns. Author's collection.

occasion. Mother's later comments about other women casting admiring glances at Dad suggest that she had from the first found him physically appealing, though she once told Ruth that Dad's elegant table manners had been the initial attraction.

Busy though she was during the Goodland years, Mother paid attention to her looks. I recall a bedtime ceremony of braiding her hair, applying cold cream, and rubbing the back of her hands over her upraised neck to reduce a threatening double chin. To me, of course, she just looked like Mama. The heat and smell of her physical presence meant more to me than her appearance. When I snuggled up, I could inhale her reassuring aroma of Ivory soap and sweat with something mysteriously animal underneath. At movies she would sometimes reach over and hold my hand in scenes that she thought might upset me. Once, on a hot day after a long dinner, she asked me to remove my head from her lap. The rejection was painful.

I liked best of all the combination of physical and verbal communication when, in bed before we fell asleep, with Rena on one side of Mother and me pressing against her on the other, she read aloud. Sometimes the book was *Mother's Story of the Bible*, short tales with garish illustrations. Sometimes it was *David Copperfield*, which put me to sleep after a page or two. We never got to the end.

In our daytime interaction, when begged for permission to do something, Mother would occasionally reply, "Ask your father." Generally, however, she made the decisions in domestic, social, and educational matters. Sometimes at night I could hear my parents in bed together exchanging what seemed to be counsel on family matters. After her death, in 1968, my father incessantly recalled what a fine mind she had and how steadily she applied it to the family's well-being. At that point he did not recall her compulsively clean and tidy housekeeping, which earlier he had complained of, blaming it on the year she had lived with a rigid widowed sister of her deceased father, a mysterious "Aunt Em Boyer."

Her own mother, though no obsessive housekeeper, was a great manager. Left a widow with eight children, five of them still at home, she had kept Indian Hill Farm going and become a leader in school and community affairs. She was "Grandmother Eddy" to many folks who were not relatives. She and Dad had great respect for each other, the very opposite of mother-in-law versus son-in-law stereotypes. The contrast with his own gentle but rather ineffectual mother probably inspired his admiration.

Grandmother Eddy took the lead in making the match between her daughter and Jim Hawkins. "How did Daddy propose?" we used to query my parents. They put us off, and once Mother said she just didn't remember. Many years later he confessed to me that there was no proposal. The two women had simply begun talking about a good date for the wedding and the convenience of having the couple live with Grandmother Eddy, who was turning the farm over to a son and moving into Topeka. Her house would be close enough to the telegraph office for Dad to walk to work.

Married in March, Mother was pregnant six months later, and Dean was born the day before her twentieth birthday. But even while the family grew, she continued as a self-educator, interested in the news, fond of books, and active in women's clubs. Because Dad suffered eyestrain from his night work, he usually settled for the headlines. In their later years, she often read to him.

She wanted us to have good table manners and to speak good English. Although she made fun of those who referred to women's legs as "limbs," I never heard her use the word "stink." Things had "an unpleasant odor." With people outside the family circle, she was cordial but reserved. Her older brothers liked to kid her about having enough dignity for the whole family.

Her attention to good manners made it all the more fun when she let her hair down at home. She didn't like board games, but would let me draw her into word games and challenge her with riddles. At a revealing slip of the tongue (often beyond my comprehension), she laughed as heartily as anyone at the table. She could make fun of the bloomers she was wearing in the old photograph of the Washburn Academy girls' basketball team.

One evening, after Helene demonstrated that she could stand on her head, we pleaded with Mother to back up the claim we had heard from Dad that she could write with her toes. Off came her shoe and stocking to let her grasp a pencil between her big and second toes. In large, shaky, but quite legible letters she wrote her name. "But don't ever tell anyone," she cautioned.

In middle age my parents made a strikingly handsome couple. Her hair stayed dark, his was "prematurely gray" (actually white), complementing his ruddy complexion. Fretting about other women's envy, she admonished her children that if she died first, they must protect him from any threatening vamp. "Make sure he marries a nice woman like Mrs. Poland."

Although Mother sometimes addressed him as "Father" and referred to him when talking to her children as "your father," to his children he was "Papa" or "Daddy." For me he became "Dad" only in later life, when I decided that "Daddy" was an infantile regionalism. Mother's occasional references to "Jim," in conversations with older friends, gave a tantalizing hint of parental intimacy, but their kiss when one or the other left on a trip was disappointingly chaste.

In railroad memoranda, which, like many of his colleagues, he brought home for use as scratch paper, he was designated "JAH." He signed his checks "J. A. Hawkins."

Mother signed hers "Mrs. J. A. Hawkins." The *A* stood for Adam, the name of his German grandfather, but he disliked it and occasionally used "Adams" instead.

Family policy held that to avoid wasting paper all letters should cover each page completely. Accordingly, Dad's one surviving letter from Goodland, January 10, 1936, midway in the year of separation, brims with homey detail. He reports Dean's raise at the packing plant and Ruth's volleyball practice, his success in getting his shoes half-soled and the price of a round roast Dean had brought home (11¢ a pound), as well as his own current weight of 180 pounds, down from 195 at Thanksgivingtime. He reflects that it would be wise to sell the Emporia farm and buy "baby bonds," whose low par value made them available to small investors. But then he adds the disconcerting thought that he might have to turn to farming if he lost his railroad job after a rumored government takeover. The letter ends with a wistful declaration that "Dean and Ruth" think Mother can rent the Herington house soon and that we can all be living together again.

My mother comes back in these early memories as an active, speaking presence, a source of moral precept and information about the world. For the most part, my father hovers as part of the setting. Not until his eighties, when he lived with me for months at a time, did I truly come to know him. I learned then that he felt indebted to my mother for bearing a child at thirty-nine and took pride in having a second son. That he mostly left me to the attention of others had much to do with his helping his older son build back after his "nervous breakdown."

The year when the family was divided between Goodland and Herington left its mark. Although I later learned that my father frequently came to Herington, even sacrificing salary by taking time off, I have no recollections of such visits. Even when the family was living together, he had to get much of his sleep during the day. He usually worked the second trick (4 P.M. to midnight) or the third (midnight to 8 A.M.). Mother claimed that it was an advantage to have him home during the day, but his sudden appearances after napping, half-dressed and hair uncombed, hardly befit "the head of the family." His daytime sleeping required a family policy of holding the noise down. The result was encouragement of table games and reading, and a child's extra naps were never frowned on. "The time to sleep is when you're sleepy" became a family slogan.

Although he did not smoke, he shared his office with cigar smokers. Tobacco odor clung to his clothes, even the gray worsted that he reserved for formal occasions. Mother viewed this as a misfortune to be borne. Yet the cigar smell, acrid though it was, stimulated in me a sense of a mysterious male world where things domestically forbidden could occur.

When he had his day off or worked third trick, Dad would be home at bedtime. With goodnight kisses in order, I sometimes insisted on skipping him since any growth of beard made his face scratchy. He only laughed. He later boasted to me about his ability to put a restless infant to sleep by walking back and forth with the child in his arms from a lighted room into a darkened one. No doubt I was cuddled that way, and I can remember later occasions when he helped me fall asleep. Lying beside me, he would count my vertebrae, starting at the neck, exerting a gentle pressure, presumably learned from his own treatments by an osteopath. After a little squirming, I found the process relaxing, almost hypnotic, with a satisfying tingle at the end as he pressed his thumbs between the tops of my buttocks, saying, "And the tailbone finishes it up."

Dad liked to go rabbit hunting with Dean, and sometimes they took me along. I never handled the shotgun, but I can remember its blast, followed usually by a fine view of the zigzagging hindquarters of a fleeing jackrabbit. Although assured it tasted like chicken, I refused to eat the occasional trophy from these expeditions. Nobody told me of the far bloodier rabbit hunts a few years earlier, when desperate farmers circled an area, drove the predators into pens, and clubbed them to death.

Dad and Dean shared a bag of golf clubs. In Herington the family had belonged to the country club. My only memories of it come from a photograph of the modest clubhouse preserved in our album and a much later letter announcing the organization's bankruptcy. Although they chose to forgo a similar club near Goodland, the two men occasionally tried out their swings on a makeshift course set up in Horace Johns's pasture. About the time I turned nine they decided to include me. In my single golfing lesson, I let my swing follow through as directed, but the club gashed my father's head behind his ear. Although he made light of the blood, it horrified me to see myself as the agent of such patricidal carnage.

Mother's confidence and her certainty of our respectability drew heavily on Dad's steady employment with the Rock Island. She expressed forebodings of being left a widow. His inflamed gall bladder had caused her a great scare. Though this was before my birth, I heard about the resulting operation because of the awe-inspiring scar on Dad's belly. When he suffered an occasional ulcer attack, sometimes so severe that he took days off, her optimism about quick recovery was not entirely convincing. Three days on a milk and egg diet generally sufficed, but he had to watch what he ate. Shredded wheat, for instance, was judged dangerously scratchy, and tomatoes too acidic.

Even with Depression-era poverty visible among some schoolmates, I never felt our family to be at risk. Still, I was curious. "How much does Daddy make?" I asked Mother one day.

She hesitated, but finally, influenced probably by some parental guide that mandated telling children the truth, informed me, "He makes ten dollars a day, but you must never tell that to anyone." This prosperity amazed me.

By comparison, Dean's answer to my query, "Are we rich or poor?" was a little disappointing. "We're neither very rich nor very poor. You could say we're right in the middle."

Dean had it right, and yet with marriageable daughters and a sense of reputability that drew on upstanding relatives in Topeka and Emporia, the family took pains with appearances. Although hard to keep polished, the two crystal chandeliers in the Fowler house were considered an advantageous amenity, as were the French doors between the living and dining rooms. Faye once told me that the first time she was invited to the house, she felt nervous because she had heard that the Hawkinses had money.

CHAPTER 6

Reaching the Rest of the World

Prior to the motor age 50 percent of local employment [in
Goodland] was furnished by the railroad; now, owing to
the decline in rail traffic, only 15 or 20 percent depend
upon this industry.

—*The WPA Guide to 1930s Kansas,* p. 335

THE WIND, it seemed, blew constantly in Goodland.
Walking between home and school, I expected either to
gain speed with it at my back or to bend into it and press
each step harder. Sometimes, trudging into the teeth of
the wind, I would turn and walk backward for a bit, just
to protect my face and catch my breath. But when the dust
swept in, the wind became a barrage. Once or twice I had
to hurry home from school with black clouds boiling up
just above the horizon. Clearer in my memory, the family
car waits to pick up Rena and me at Grant School because
of a big storm on the way.

At home I watched Mother trying to cope with the leav-
ings of storms. She had to decide if even fresh clothes must
now be returned to the washing machine. She taped the
windows to keep out the dust, but it seeped in anyway.
Rena, rather wittily I felt, brushed the dust from one window sill after a storm and enclosed it in a letter back to

Elizabeth Tripp, demonstrating the rigors of our new locale.

Dad didn't complain, but no doubt the storms upset railroad schedules. In a few cases mounds of dust reminiscent of snowdrifts brought trains to a halt. Delays meant changed meeting points and disappointing reports sent back to headquarters. And of course he had to get to work whether or not swirling dust made driving hazardous.

We knew that farmers had it worst of all. What townsfolk referred to as dust storms, farmers often called dirt storms. Old-timers' tales about fiercer storms two or three years earlier offered some consolation, as did reports in newspapers about heavier damage to farmland down toward the Oklahoma panhandle. The usual labels among professional historians for the 1930s, such as Depression Decade, the Age of Roosevelt, the Hungry Years, do not include the one most common in western Kansas—the Dirty Thirties.

All in all, the Dust Bowl era was not necessarily traumatic for a child. I liked the shared challenge that brought the family together in the face of threatening nature. Sometimes I could help by sweeping the sidewalk after the storm passed, and it was no great price to pay if I had to wash my face more often and clean out my nose with the little cloth squares and boric-acid water that Mother set up for us in the bathroom.

If I found comfort in thinking of Goodland as only a temporary home, it was far less because of the dust storms, which abated after 1937, than because of anticipations of a better life elsewhere, anticipations encouraged by radio programs, cars, movies, and of course trains, especially ones to take us far away on Dad's free passes.

Although I knew it had importance as the county seat for Sherman County, I thought of Goodland as a railroad town. Its center was not a courthouse square, but Main

Street, long and broad, leading to a group of railroad buildings—the depot, the freight house, the office building. The tinplated grain elevator seemed their adjunct, a link to the outlying farms.

Dad's connection to a corporation greater than local businesses, one that advertised in magazines, reassured me. Only rarely did I see him in his office. Looking serious and wearing his green eyeshade, he worked at a long table with lined "train sheets" spread out before him. Train numbers with arrival and departure times were inscribed there in his angular but legible hand. Some of the train orders and other messages, typed on yellow half sheets, bore the impressive signature "JAH." That these initials meant my father to railroad men up and down the line seemed to me a highly desirable sort of reputation. If it weren't for his calculations about sidings and meeting points, there would be terrible train accidents. That I knew.

When Dad's schedule allowed him to be at the dinner table with us, especially on his day off, he would talk about his work. Only Mother took much of it in. Any report of a derailment or washout stirred my interest, and I vaguely understood what "maintenance of way" and "hot-shot" referred to, but was happy to have conversation turn to other matters.

In his cheery way, Dad maintained that train dispatching was just like a game. Indeed, I ultimately concluded that many of his fellow dispatchers similarly had little formal education (Dad's, in a one-room school, ended with the seventh grade), but that, like him, they found fulfillment in a mentally demanding job. After nostalgia for the vanishing railroads set in, a game called Train Dispatcher appeared on the market. Rena heard about it in the early 1970s, and we contemplated giving a set to our recently widowed father. But we soon decided he could find more satisfaction in his memories than in this simulation.

The names of railroads other than the Rock Island peppered Dad's conversation, especially when he was proposing a vacation trip with foreign passes. We heard most often about the Santa Fe (pronounced "Santa Fee" in my Goodland memories). At the beginning of his railroad career, Dad worked with that company as a signal operator and station agent, and Mother's oldest brother, Quincy, worked in the Santa Fe's Topeka shops as a machinist.

Stopped at a crossing to wait for a long freight train to pass, we amused ourselves by spotting boxcars from other lines, figuring out what the various initials stood for, and wondering why a freight car from as far away as the Boston & Maine would have reached western Kansas. We marveled at the longest freights, especially when pulled by two engines, a "double-header."

Sometimes Dad took the family car to the office, but more often Dean or Ruth would drive him to work and pick him up. At times I was sent along for the ride. The more of us in the car, the happier Mother was, perhaps on the theory that more passengers lowered the per capita cost of the gasoline. Rather unwillingly, I would find myself sitting in the car, looking at the rear of the railroad structures. The ground nearby was mostly cinders and weeds, the unadorned buildings boringly practical.

In more cheerful recollections, we are parked at the depot facing the platform. Sometimes we are there because a family member is arriving or departing. In those cases we have gone to the station early to see who else in town might be traveling.

Out in the car on an errand, we would sometimes drive to the depot, park, and watch the activities on the platform. Older family members would help each other identify the comers and goers. Mother would point out proper and improper travel dress. An acquaintance might come up to the car and chat through the rolled-down window.

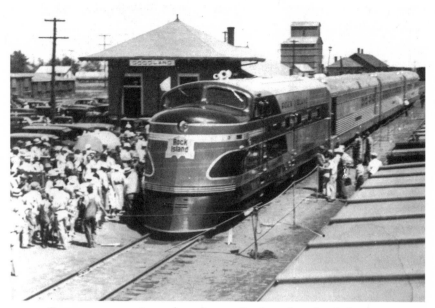

Our passes weren't good on the new Rockets, *but they helped us take pride in the Rock Island. Courtesy of Parker Collection, Sherman County Historical Society.*

The individual passengers interested me moderately, but not as much as listening for the growl of the approaching train engine and then the whistle at the crossing, or watching the wheels slow or gradually build up speed on departure. Occasionally, my mother could name the engineer or the conductor. We liked conductors best. We encountered them on train trips, friendly, ready to explain why we were running late, and sometimes sending a greeting to "Jimmy."

The scene at the train station reassured us that we could connect to the rest of the world. When it was time to visit in Topeka—or to go see if California really was the Golden State—the railroad provided the network that would take us there and bring us back.

Greyhound and other busses stopped in Goodland, but I

have no memory of them. They lacked the romance of the railroad. Of course, trucks also tied us to the outside, but they were a curse. They blocked our view when we were driving on the highway. They didn't pay a fair share of taxes, my father informed us, and they broke down the road surface. Any railroader would tell you that.

Grown-ups must have warned me against playing on the tracks. I did it anyway if a companion would initiate the adventure. I remember watching two fellow trespassers place pennies on the rails, retrieve the flattened coins after a train passed, and declare these would make wonderful rings. Mostly we spent the time jumping from tie to tie, or proving we could keep our balance walking along a rail. Breathing in the pungent strangeness, we could follow the tracks out of town along the raised roadbed, where barbed wire fences kept farm animals safe and the twin rails stretched endlessly ahead, merging into a single line.

A good trophy from such a walk would be a railroad spike, worked loose from the edge of a rail, or better yet, a date nail from one of the ties. On the blunt end we would find a year marked, a record that placed the nail and us in a flow of time. I couldn't convince the other boys how important this was. My impulse to consider the past lacked the skills of a good historian.

Once, I realized, the railroad had not been here. Laying the tracks had been part of that great movement of Americans, symbolized even more impressively for me by our family's small copper replica of a covered wagon drawn by four oxen. Such a conveyance had brought Grandmother Eddy to Kansas in 1859, back when, as she liked to express it, the land was "all open prairie."

In the many interviews she gave as her longevity made her a Topeka personage, she often traced the progress she had witnessed by describing the sequence of changing means of transportation. Someday, she would winsomely add, she might go for an airplane ride herself. And at the age of ninety-nine she did that, giving the reporters yet another human-interest story.

Though the Rock Island was in bankruptcy protection, and Dad sounded unhappy when he mentioned it, he also spoke confidently of reorganization and of Farrington, the new man at the top. Dad had met John D. Farrington and shared his optimistic view that the newly purchased diesel engines would help put the company back in the black. Even better news came when the Rock Island began to advertise itself as "The Route of the *Rockets*." The magazine pictures and the posters that displayed these beautiful, sleek streamliners were at least as alluring as the latest automobile ads.

Our passes weren't good on the *Rockets*, but we still took pride in them. Much of the town turned out to see the *Rocky Mountain Rocket* on its initial run through Good-

The candles on Grandmother Eddy's birthday cake became unmanageable even before her last birthday, at age 107. Author's collection.

land in November 1939. The physical presence of the trains made it easy to dream of worlds far from Goodland.

Radio stirred the imagination in a different way. Jokes borrowed from radio programs spiced the conversation of my friends, and I am sure most Goodland families had a radio. Oddly, the Hawkinses did not. We had had a large console radio in Herington. The manuscript census returns for 1930—the year the census ventured for the first time into quality-of-life matters and asked about radio ownership—show that almost all our neighbors along South C Street also had a set. Although reception on the console was often staticky, I can remember listening there with Rena to "her program," *Little Orphan Annie.*

By sending in the required Ovaltine labels and some money, she acquired a decoder pin. When Annie and companions were surrounded by flames at the end of one episode, Rena was able to work out the coded secret that foretold their rescue. Annie's dog, Sandy, would carry out a message and bring help.

We brought the console radio to Goodland, but the reception declined. Before long, the receiver and speaker were removed and the cabinet used for storage. Why my parents didn't—as they would have put it—"invest" in another radio, I can only surmise. Not spending the money (the "Scotch" in us) was part of the motivational mix. But in their private counsels, they may have decided that radio meant wasted time and put shallow ideas into their children's heads.

Was it parental uneasiness about this deprivation that brought permission for me to use the car radio? I sat in the car for half an hour most weekday afternoons listening to "my programs." Of *Jack Armstrong, the All-American Boy*, I can remember chiefly the rousing high-school song that opened each episode, although doubtless Jack's manliness and the warm camaraderie appealed to me. Because

Easy Aces followed *Jack Armstrong*, I began listening to that also. Though not directed at children, the program offered broad humor easy to appreciate. Jane Ace, the dopey, malaprop-spouting wife, constantly exasperated her husband, but usually found vindication in the closing moments. A half hour was all I was allowed. More would have threatened that dreaded automotive disaster, a run-down battery.

The odd circumstance of having a radio in the car but not in the house helped inspire weekend afternoon drives, another way to leave Goodland behind. These outings usually included the whole family, though my sisters sometimes begged off. As we traversed the flat dirt roads with their deep ditches, one tedious mile to the next corner, we listened to serious music, courtesy of the Texaco opera broadcasts or the *Bell Telephone Hour*. Names like Lily Pons and Lawrence Tibbett stayed with us, associated with art and fame. Once we timed our drive specifically to hear Winston Churchill. The sonorous address delighted us with its disdainful pronunciation of the word "Nazi."

Far more than just the location of our radio, the car provided a way to traverse the borders of our small town. Mother tried to stir interest in the landscape, urging Rena and me to look for the next windmill or to notice snow fences that had just been put up. She had us compete to spot the scattered hillocks of a prairie-dog town. But I found the tumbleweeds most engaging. They seemed like fast-moving animals, threatening even when caught in the barbed wire. After deciding they were not alive, I had touched one once and knew that they had their own barbs.

Having grown up on farms, my parents could usually guess what was planted in each field, even if green barely showed. I never learned the identifying marks, but strange crop names—timothy, broomcorn, milo—linger in my mind. The grown-ups offered a running commentary that compared local farming prospects unfavorably to those of eastern Kansas, sometimes declaring that it would be better to let this rain-deprived area go back to buffalo grass. (Only years later did I realize the obvious appeal to land-seeking farmers of an area with no trees to remove and no frustrating slopes or hills.) Marion Talley, the opera singer, had bought acreage out here, we heard, misled by the evanescent green of the fields one early spring. A mysterious "dry farming" might or might not rescue the region.

Occasionally the declared goal of the drive was the "old soddy," supposedly the only sod house left in the county. Its walls, blocks of dried turf, still stood, though the roof had vanished along with the hopes of the original settler. We explored its yard and interior, but no relics of its inhabitants turned up.

When we packed a lunch and drove to "the grove," we made the best of this rare patch of skimpy shade, where some government agency had planted trees and provided a picnic table. We thought longingly of gatherings in "the timber," an imposing cluster of cottonwoods at Indian Hill Farm, the setting for Eddy family Fourth-of-July reunions. Admittedly, western Kansas had magnificent sunsets, and sometimes, as we headed back to Goodland, we simply stopped the car to take in the vivid play of pinks against the deepening blue.

The two cars we bought in Goodland, first a Chrysler and then a Buick, far surpassed the old Marquette, though I always recalled it fondly. Its protruding door hinges had let me climb through a window when I couldn't yet open the door. Both the newer cars had curved silhouettes, chrome trim, and subtle colors. On our family drives, the technique of the driver, usually Dean, and the car's interior interested me more than the landscape. My father had had the cigarette lighter removed (a temptation, he said), but the dashboard still offered a full display of magical equipment. By watching the odometer closely, I could announce to everybody the exact moment the mileage would go up by one. Dean would alert me when a row of zeros was about to appear.

In retrospect I am surprised at how readily the folks let the car be used when my sisters and their friends participated in a choral contest or attended a school ball game in a neighboring town, such as Colby, our great rival. Dean would drive on these occasions, and it was on one of them, when a flat tire delayed the return trip, that he and Faye began their romance.

Nothing carried us away like the movies. Despite our parents' concern that the products of Hollywood had a bad influence on the young, the Jeanette MacDonald-Nelson Eddy films proved irresistible. The whole family went, and we saw them all, beginning with *Naughty Marietta*. Ruth even bought the sheet music for some of its songs.

Mother was born an Eddy, and the thought of some faint family connection to the star dissolved any initial doubts about these musicals. Disappointingly, Nelson turned out to be an extremely distant relative, as research in "the Eddy book" made clear. This vast genealogical compendium had been purchased soon after Mother tracked down the record of Samuel Eddy, whose patriotic soldiering permitted her entry into the Daughters of the American Revolution. Many years later, I was surprised to hear her refer to the lack of "music" in Nelson's voice and the woodenness of his acting. Unmusical though I was, his resounding baritone fixed melodies in my head that I found myself humming weeks later.

Dad rarely accompanied us to the movies, in part because he was usually at the office in the evening. Perhaps more than Mother he was wary of the effect of movies on their children. In one of our few confidential conversations during the Goodland years, he told me of the first movie he had seen. It started by showing the hero lying down under a tree and falling asleep. What followed was understood to be his dream. "So always think of the movie that way," he counseled. "It isn't real life. It's somebody's dream." Of course he was right, but it was easy to make some dreams my own.

In Herington, where the theater was named the Dreamland, my parents had at least once casually sent me along with my sisters to the movies, probably believing me, at five or six years old, too young to understand the content. They were wrong. Two images stayed with me. One presented Bruno Hauptman in a flickering newsreel as he awaited execution. Would he or wouldn't he confess to killing the Lindbergh baby? The other was a scene from a murder mystery. The crucial clue depended on the right- or left-handedness of the victim. We sat through much of the movie twice, as allowed in those casual days, to see if the victim had indeed held the cup of poisoned coffee in her left hand. This focus on "evidence" made me particularly attentive to the sprawled corpse, which I can still conjure up all these years later.

In Goodland I was told that certain movies would be "too grown-up" for me. That judgment seemed to apply to all Bette Davis films. Still, I can remember my sisters discussing the plot of *Jezebel* and my mother declaring that it gave a good example of how not to behave. Why was I taken along to see so grown-up a film as *Becky Sharp*? Perhaps because it was touted as a Technicolor first. Perhaps because its source in *Vanity Fair* connected it to good literature. Once I saw a movie simply because Ruth gained permission to go out on this particular date only by promising to take Hughie along. With the decency to be embarrassed, I played dumb during the pair's cryptic romantic conversation.

For Goodland's Sherman Theatre, the British spelling

The Sherman Theatre. We never sat in the reserved seats, but for a nickel the Saturday double feature filled the afternoon. Courtesy of Branda Inc.

provided the only touch of elegance, other than the reserved section—two rows of leather seats, an optimum distance from the screen and set off by velvet ropes. We never paid the higher price required. Rena and I eagerly awaited the Sherman's monthly calendar, anticipating which films we would get to see and hoping to learn the names of any new stars. With four different films per week (five if you counted the Saturday double feature) we had plenty to choose from, but of course we didn't attend all we hoped to. Whenever Mother kept us from seeing one that was sure to be the talk of our friends, we found no comfort in her stock consolation: "If it's any good, it will come back."

With the news that a movie would be made in Goodland, rumors spread and dreams swelled. Who would be in it? Would it be widely shown? Perhaps the film company was scouting for talent. Scoffers belittled it all as a promotional effort by the Sherman Theatre.

Posters in store windows announced tryouts, and within

a month *Runnin' Wild* premiered at the Sherman. My sisters took me along, going early to make sure we could find seats.

In the opening shot, Cherry Roberts, the town's best twirler, who had won several competitions, manipulated her baton with dazzling speed. The cameraman, however, had concentrated on her legs. Gladys Adams (Dean's "nightowl") had a leading role. The plot, so far as I can recall, involved the theft of jewelry during the distraction of Cherry's performance. Portrayed by two high-school football players, the thieves skulked down an alley, then, in the shelter of a railroad embankment, examined their loot. The camera showed them ogling a pearl necklace pulled from a satchel. Their capture by a uniformed policeman brought the spectacle to an abrupt end.

In spite of the locals' laughter and applause, I felt let down. The film was silent, lasted well under half an hour, and a few shots cut off the tops of actors' heads. Whoever these filmmakers were, they didn't represent the real Hollywood. In movies, and maybe in every field, it made little sense to wait in one's hometown to be discovered.

Our very enthusiasm may have worried our parents. Perhaps they knew, at least by title, the disquieting psychological survey *Our Movie Made Children*, and sometimes they heard the minister refer to Hollywood immorality. On the whole, at our house anti-movie strictures remained mild. Once or twice, however, my misbehavior brought the threat, "Hughie, if you're going to act that way after you see a movie, you can't go to any more." This struck me as unfair. Whatever I had done seemed utterly unrelated to anything I had watched on the screen.

Without question I was old enough for any Shirley Temple film. The love-hate reaction that she evoked in most of my generation has persisted. If at our age she was a movie star, why shouldn't we be movie stars? Someone gave me her purported autobiography, a Big-Little book with photographs on every other page. After reading it, I could see that simply being in the right part of California had been crucial to her success, and I began to feel sorry for her, taught alone with one teacher instead of in a regular school class.

I attended her films at every opportunity. Of course it wasn't real life, but I couldn't help crying in *Bright Eyes* when her mother died, struck by an automobile while hurrying along with a big package under her arm. When opened, the package turned out to contain a big airplane-shaped birthday cake meant for Shirley. We learned many of Shirley's songs. A chum and I spent a long time one Saturday playing outside the Christian Church, singing "On the Good Ship Lollipop." At the final phrase, "Happy landings on a chocolate bar," we let ourselves slide down the cement drainway that ran alongside the church steps. If we slipped, we added, "Oops, it was rotten." Honest recollection requires me to admit that my friend initiated this addendum. Still, I recognized its wit and quickly took it up.

My unvoiced resentment of Shirley made it comforting to hear Mother say, "I think she overacts," and to learn that Rena preferred Shirley's mean little counterpart, Jane Withers.

We felt no such antagonism to Judy Garland, who breathed new life into the Hardy family series. Not only did I remember all the songs she sang in *The Wizard of Oz*, which I saw twice in a row, but I memorized most of the dialogue. I reimagined the scenario scene by scene, trying fruitlessly to figure out how we could present it as a puppet show.

For five cents, any parent could send a child off to a long Saturday afternoon in the popcorn-scented staleness of the Sherman Theatre. Although almost no adults attended, the auditorium remained orderly. Whispering subsided as we accepted whatever the glittering screen offered. But we had our favorites. Applause greeted the cartoons, loudest for those from Looney Tunes. Besides the cartoon, previews of coming attractions, a newsreel, and a serial enhanced the scheduled double feature. In the predictably plotted Westerns, leading men were hard to tell apart, except for Gene Autry, but their sidekicks, such as Smiley Burnette and George "Gabby" Hayes, proved memorably individual, funny, and often shrewd.

If the crime-and-prison films threatened youthful psyches, my parents never knew because they never saw them. I liked them far better than the Westerns. The yearning of prisoners to break free had a special appeal no matter how evil the deed that had got them locked up. Recognizing what I considered a deep insight into the role of chance in setting a life's direction, I could never forget Pat O'Brien's closing line, "Let's go and say a prayer for a boy who couldn't run as fast as I could."

Sometimes the serial provided the main motive for returning the next Saturday. How could the hero or his girlfriend possibly escape the catastrophe looming at the end of the last installment? Would the converging ships crush the rowboat? Could the fall from the cliff end short of the rocks below? Sometimes the deliverance proved ingenious, but often it relied on a cheap trick by inserting a few frames of film just before the crisis. To me, this suppressing of evidence constituted cheating. Gradually the serials lost their appeal. Anyway, if I missed an episode, friends eagerly explained what had saved the day.

Goodland offered a child a good life, but I never imagined I would stay there. Trains and cars could carry me out of town, maybe some day for good, and radio and movies showed me a wider world. Other places beckoned. If some lay in a dreamy unreality over the rainbow, there must be others that I could reach before too long.

CHAPTER 7

At Our House

Aluminum will make your cooking faster, tastier, and
more nutritious.

—Wearever salesman

§OME PEOPLE date events by pregnancies, others by
World Series rivalries or major elections. None of these
devices works well for childhood memories. Often I can
determine the year of an event because of the house in
which it occurred. Places come back to mind as dates
do not. The recollections that I can locate in the Kimmel
house, often in specific rooms, I know are those of a seven-
year-old. It was in the living room that Rena refused to
read *Jane Arden* to me. In the kitchen I was caught in my
trial fib, saying I had washed my face when I hadn't. We sat
at the dining-room table as we read the results of handwriting samples we had sent to a character analyst. ("Mr.
Hawkins, your handwriting suggests immaturity, but this is
perhaps because of your youth.")

Mrs. Kimmel's rangy bungalow with its big yard, shady
by Goodland standards, stood on a corner, a setting that
added to its appeal. We settled in there after the hurried
move from Herington in September 1936. Unlike the
Cherry Street house, which never lost its feeling of imper-
manence, the Kimmel house, though also a rental, some-

how counted as home. Attending Grant School made that clear.

We would not be returning to our own house in Herington, now in the hands of more dependable tenants.

The Kimmel house neighbors I remember best, the Euwers, lived on the corner diagonally across, in a much newer house. Elmer Euwer, an influential lawyer and politician, had in fact attended Washburn Academy in Topeka with my mother. Dad mischievously let it slip that Mr. Euwer was an old beau of hers. She pooh-poohed the idea, but when we teased her about it, she simply smiled.

Mistakenly thinking her younger than I was, I considered it somewhat demeaning to play with the Euwers's daughter, Eloise. My sisters declared her particularly beautiful, a rare combination of brown eyes and blond hair. This added nothing to her appeal for me. I found her rather spoiled, but nevertheless enjoyed sharing the expensive new games she got at Christmas.

In our family's dinner-table conversation, the Euwers were cited as models of good citizenship. At Thanksgiving Mrs. Euwer brought over a mincemeat pie. We all declared it delicious, made even more special when Mother confided that she thought there was brandy in it. Kansas was a dry state, of course, and we heard only good things about Carrie Nation, who braved jail in her battle against the saloons. Still, only an extremist would object to following an old family recipe that called for a little brandy.

Because Mrs. Kimmel needed her house back, we moved in mid-1937 to the east side of town, to the Fowler house. Laid off by the Rock Island, Mr. Fowler had found a better job in Denver on what my father called the "Deenargee." (In time I deciphered this insider code for the Denver & Rio Grande Western Railroad.) Mrs. Fowler had "good taste." Her touches of elegance included crystal chandeliers and bathroom fixtures like those in current magazine ads. Of more practical importance for a family our size, the full basement offered an extra bedroom.

Newer than the Kimmel house, the Fowlers' lacked large trees. Wanting to teach me the nature of chores, Dad had me water the two young Chinese elms in the front yard, both already bent by the prevailing west wind. I would happily fill the troughs he had dug around them, taking care to avoid wasteful overflow. While instructing me in this process, Dad also showed me how to take a drink from a hose by kinking it to create a manageable stream.

The Fowlers' backyard included a goldfish pond. We stocked it twice, both times with rapidly fatal results. Somewhat more successful was the long vegetable garden that stretched to the end of the property. I recall harvesting at least onions and horseradish. Although Dad had planted a garden regularly in Herington, this was his only such venture in Goodland. A father-son snapshot shows us posed rigidly side by side in the apparently neglected garden. Dad had suggested to the photographer, probably Ruth, that we should be recorded busily weeding, but she declared we were too neatly dressed for that to be credible.

Our neighbors made the Fowler house even more congenial. On the lot behind us, facing the next street, the Fowlers' son-in-law operated the greenhouse where I had obtained the name for an x flower. In a one-room cabin on the alley lived Alberto, a sweet-tempered immigrant from the Philippines who helped in the greenhouse, having come to Goodland on some railroad project. My family spoke positively of his good manners. A snapshot of him, proudly standing by his door, helped keep his memory alive in later years.

Next door lived Mrs. Fowler's parents, Mr. and Mrs. Robbins, who had given her part of their vast lot for the house we now rented. Their gabled house with its big stone front porch dominated the block. Intimidatingly robust for

*At the Fowler house, the railwayman is just up from his nap, about
to leave for the office. His son is proud to be photographed with
Daddy. Author's collection.*

a septuagenarian and usually wordless, Mr. Robbins had occupied his retirement years filling their side yard with objects of stone and mortar—benches, ponds arched by bridges, and birdbaths edged with colored glass. As neighbors, we had free access to their yard swing. Sometimes I swung there with playmates. Sometimes in the evening Mother and I would sit there chatting with Mrs. Robbins.

Vigorous and competent, Mrs. Robbins reminded us of Grandmother Eddy. Occasionally she called me in to eat cookies at her dining-room table. Everything in the shadowed room seemed out of another age, and I tried not to stare at the monstrous oak sideboard. During one of our heart-to-heart conversations, Mrs. Robbins assured me: "I never call them 'niggers.'" Deeply impressed, I vowed that I never would either.

She kept chickens, and sometimes after amusing myself among the stonework, I returned home with a gift of fresh eggs. For our part, we contributed to the health of the poultry with our kitchen scraps. I would carry the refuse to the alley and toss it over the wire fence into the pen, waiting to watch the scrambling chickens compete for tidbits. Even garbage had its uses, and Mrs. Robbins assured us that we could include eggshells, which provided something that the chickens craved. This element of their diet I found unsettlingly cannibalistic.

The near-bliss of this neighborliness collapsed one Saturday afternoon when Mr. Robbins came bursting into our kitchen, red in the face. "It's Nelly! It's Nelly! Something's wrong." Older family members rushed next door, leaving me bewildered, frightened by the anguish of my stolid neighbor but telling myself nothing really bad could have happened.

The stroke had been instantly fatal, and I heard the not-very-consoling words, "She did not have to suffer." Two days later as the family drove to the funeral home I begged to see Mrs. Robbins once more, but no, I was too young and must stay in the car.

Afterward we tried to be good neighbors to Mr. Robbins. We took him with us on a family trip to Denver so that he could spend a day with his daughter. On the way he lit a cigar, a male prerogative never before asserted in our car. The whole procedure was new to me. As his ash extended, I kept opening the car ashtray as a hint of approaching disaster. Dean told me to stop pestering and let Mr. Robbins enjoy his cigar.

On the return trip, after darkness settled and with Dean at the wheel, the car skidded on the graveled road and tilted into a ditch. Although asleep before the accident, I took pride in being the first to notice that Dean's forehead was bleeding. As we waited to hear about repairs and get a loaner for the rest of the trip, the folks insisted Dean go to a local doctor. Returning, he assured us it was nothing. The doctor had applied a small bandage and told him his bruises were worse injuries than the cut.

In the aftermath, Mother consulted my sisters on just how to report the accident in a letter to Mrs. Fowler without alarming her. After opening thanks for the hospitality in her lovely Denver home came the last paragraph, which Ruth and Rena judged to be just right: "We did have a bit of a spill on the way home. Some loose gravel put us into the ditch, but no one was hurt. Your father was asleep. He told us later with a twinkle in his eye, "Next time I'll stay awake and not miss the excitement." He had indeed made that comment, but the twinkling eye was pure poetic license.

The Fowlers had left some of their furniture, which we integrated with pieces brought from Herington. The house there was left "partially furnished" on the theory that one got better tenants if they had their own furniture. Much of ours was Mission oak, shipped in parts years before from Grand Rapids. Even older was the winged leather rocking chair, in which all the children had been rocked as babies. Now Mother sat there as she did the family mending.

The dining room served as the family gathering place. Along with the rocker, the daybed provided comfortable seating. Its rounded ends of pierced metal made fascinating patterns on the wall when the sun hit them directly. Anyone reading or writing usually sat at the round oak table. Earlier, and possibly even in the Fowler house, I had played in the fortress of legs beneath the table, finding delight in a space that fit me but not the grown-ups.

If callers came they sat in the living room. I have fleeting memories of several such formal occasions. The enthralling Southern accent of one visitor echoes in my recollection of her startling avowal, "I just know the good Lord did not mean for us to eat duck." On his way through town, Hugh Bryden dropped in. He had taught my father telegraphy after convincing the teenage farmer that his hard outdoor labor was profitless. Having been named for this man, I was disappointed when he accepted the presence of his namesake with a perfunctory pat on the head.

Mostly, the closed French doors kept living and dining rooms separate. Nobody forbade me to play in the living room, but it had little appeal. My sisters sometimes used it as a refuge, Ruth to work on her manicure, Rena to read a book.

Any pictures on the walls were ours, not the Fowlers'. We had left some in the Herington attic, and years passed before I saw again the vaguely remembered broken Indian in *The End of the Trail* or the quotation from Phillips Brooks, framed with a photograph of his benign, beefy face. But of course we took the Sandzen "original" to Goodland and gave it pride of place in the living room. Mother had purchased this etching, *Prairie Pond*, in Herington when the Swedish-born Kansas artist gave a lecture before her women's club.

At the other extreme of tastefulness, a small mirror and thermometer, a promotional item from Dean's employer, showed a bosomy woman in a loose negligee holding a telephone receiver. Since its inscription read, "Calling O. K. Packing Company," I teased Dean with the suggestion that the picture showed Faye trying to reach him. Mother disapproved of the exposed cleavage but, admitting the practicality of the item, allowed it to be hung near the kitchen door.

Although who slept where on any given night remained somewhat arbitrary—at least it was so for me—the front bedroom was identified as my parents', distinguished by their walnut bedroom set, the source of considerable pride. The top of the chiffonier was so high I could barely reach it, the dressing table mirror the biggest in the house. The grain of the bed's looming headboard formed animal eyes and claws, if you used a little imagination. Sick with an ear infection, I spent two days in this bed, delightfully pampered and finding nothing but pleasure when Mother administered the soothing warm eardrops.

What we called our Oriental rug, probably a Belgian import, graced the living room. When an Electrolux salesman called, it was here that he showed us the marvels of his modern machine, even dropping coins on the rug and vacuuming them up. He then removed them from the dust bag, as he proved how much dirt had hidden in our supposedly clean rug. To my surprise, the combination of his charm and the demonstrated efficiency of the product succeeded. We bought the Electrolux, stopped beating rugs, and retired our faithful old upright. It now sat in the basement, its huge ballooning dust bag limp, still exuding odors of long-vanished carpets. Another antique cleaning tool, a wooden air pump designed to blow dust out of hard-to-reach corners, had fallen into disuse long before. Back in Herington it had made a fine toy for me, but it had of course been left behind in the attic and was never seen again.

The purchase of our Wearever pots and pans involved an even more memorable encounter with a sales force. To demonstrate the benefits of their aluminum cookware, a husband-and-wife team offered to prepare and serve a dinner for us and invited guests. Though not the most elegant approach to a dinner party, this painless way to entertain appealed to my mother. She had to invite at least two other couples. Faye's parents came, and so did she, in perhaps grudging recognition that she and Dean were dating. Mr. and Mrs. Johns rounded out the guest list.

Never in my life had I tasted such delicious food, though some credit should go to the visual magic. With all three leaves inserted, the oak table became oval instead of round. On the white linen tablecloth (I seem to remember the label "damask") sat our best china, hand painted by Helene as a teenager, and the best silverware, not sterling, but at least heavy silver plate. Exactly at the point of each table knife sparkled a goblet of water and ice cubes. The goblets had come as a great bargain when the local gift and jewelry store went bankrupt.

The post-dinner demonstration, part of the agreement, compared the heating time of a rod of aluminum with one of steel. Aha! The aluminum, with its higher conductivity, cooked the food faster, thus saving fuel and heightening flavor. The sales pitch went quickly, leaving plenty of time for pleasant conversation. None of the guests bought anything, but my concern for the hardworking sales folks was assuaged when Mother declared she would buy the full set.

This lively social event was a rarity. With no radio, the house in the evening could be very quiet, especially if we were all reading. In our shared devotion to books I often followed my sisters' choices. Ruth hurried through *Gone with the Wind*, which she had to return to the library in three days, having taken her turn on the waiting list. I read the opening page myself but then gave up.

Rena checked out *Chip, of the Flying U*, and I dutifully read it, impressed by the cowboys' jargon (they made fun of a woman who pronounced "chaps" the way it was written) but indignant when the heroes were killed: the Western movies never ended that way. Rena also read most of Zane Grey, but her favorite was Randall Parrish, especially his Civil War romances, *My Lady of the North* and *My Lady of the South*. Both featured interregional love affairs that overcame wartime bitterness. She owned her own copies.

Dean often bought the *Reader's Digest* downtown, but he subscribed to the *Saturday Evening Post*. Though its stories were beyond me, I pondered the illustrations and their captions. I read any ad designed like a comic strip (such as the Postum ads, with their dependable foiling of the diabolical Mr. Coffee Nerves).

The cartoons scattered through the magazine tantalized me, even when I could not see the joke. Sometimes I asked for explanations. Years later, I was surprised to find a box of these cartoons, carefully cut out with my explanatory comments inked on the back. In one, a bitter wife putting on her makeup by candlelight says to the frowning husband, "How long are you going to keep up your fight with the electric company?" On the back I found my gloss (meant to impress or help . . . whom?): "He hadn't paid the bill." Some cartoons preserved in that box came from *Farmer's Wife*, a Capper publication based in Topeka. One showed a giant federal dam project, with a harried farmer nearby assuring his wife, "Jenny, all I asked for was seeds!" The implied critique of New Deal programs was beyond me. This item remained unglossed, as did another that I puzzled over, but that nobody would interpret for me. A couple in evening clothes stand in a hotel lobby near the elevator. The man says to his surprised-looking companion, "Wait here. I'll bring the etchings down."

Cutting out pictures and saving them was a family habit.

Dean had his automobile ad collection. Rena inspired me with her scrapbook of movie-star portraits. Each bore an annotation. "She is one of my favorites" (Janet Gaynor), or, bluntly, "I have never seen or heard of her" (some minor starlet). Though not pasting them into a scrapbook, Rena collected the one-panel cartoons of Tillie the Toiler. The captions suggested a certain worldliness in the smartly dressed Tillie. In fact, fashion design may have been the true attraction of the series.

Tillie's little sister appeared increasingly in the drawings, and Rena submitted her choice in a contest to give the youngster a name. She offered Amy. Though it didn't win, Rena had greater success in a more consequential venture into nomenclature. A few years later, after we left Goodland, I found a neatly composed list she had made of attractive given names to go with the surname of her boyfriend. Over time she bestowed these names one by one on their five children.

Two of the magazines that arrived regularly had no appeal for the younger generation, the *Christian Herald*, subscribed to under pressure from the church ladies, and the *Pathfinder*, printed on low-grade pulp paper and presenting, I'm pretty sure, a Republican slant on the week's news. But *Household*, though mostly of no interest, included the irresistible Little Brown Koko stories. In these, the wide-eyed young hero naïvely succeeded amid various misadventures, which sometimes included his intriguingly named teacher, Miz Hawkins.

Crossword puzzles seemed too difficult, though their structure fascinated me. Ruth and her boyfriend H. D. would fill one in together, racing against each other, initialing the answers they put in and then totaling their scores. In that game what objection could there be to sitting close together on the daybed?

When no good magazines or library books were at hand,

or when I had reread the few books I owned to the point of near memorization, I would pull down one of the twenty volumes of *The Book of Knowledge*. Huge by a child's measure, these books were awkward to hold and included much that seemed simply dull. But I liked the poems and fairy tales as well as their stylized illustrations, taken, I later learned, from earlier-published work of some of the best English illustrators. Some of those pictures are still in my head, such as one accompanying "Four and twenty black-birds / Baked in a pie." I could dependably find something delightful in any one of these volumes. They sat at a child's eye level in a low mahogany bookcase that had come free with the collection, one of the selling points when my parents had bought this symbol of learning for their family.

A similar set, the leatherette-bound *Popular Science Library*, had far less appeal. It, too, rested in a handsome bookcase, which served nicely as an end table. These books seemed unreadable to me, and I recall only one time when they were used. In the Cherry Street house, after we had all gone out on the front porch to watch an eclipse of the moon, Dean checked the series index, tracked down an explanation of eclipses, and read it aloud. Dedicated to accurate information, he bought the *World Almanac* each year. When factual questions arose in family discussions, Dean generally could provide an answer. Perhaps his boy-hood interests had inspired the purchase of the *Popular Science Library*.

Since sheet music cost more than they usually wanted to pay, Ruth and Rena prized *Popular Song Hits*, a magazine that sold for only five cents. Its pages gave the full lyrics of songs whose melodies they might know from a movie or a friend's radio, but for which they lacked the precise words. Mother did not quite approve of these purchases. The real purpose of the love songs, she maintained, was to get young people romantically excited so that they would marry, have children, and increase national consumption. Still, she seemed to recall with pleasure the popular songs of a decade or so earlier. In Herington she sometimes sang me to sleep with "When I Grow Too Old to Dream." I remember starting to cry when I finally grasped the meaning of "And so let us part." She had to reassure me that the parting was probably just for a little while.

Through my sisters I learned the latest games of repartee. For a time, a new "knock-knock" exchange surfaced every day. Most I've forgotten, and a few were over my head.

"Knock-knock."

"Who's there?"

"Minerva."

"Minerva who?"

"'M I nevah gonna get rid of you?"

It was always risky to play, since the final comeback usually insulted the second player. The presumably witty ripostes to "What does Confucius say?" escape me now, driven out of my mind perhaps by the banal lyrics of a derivative popular song.

Ego made "T. L." a favorite verbal exchange. The intriguing initials stood for "Trade Last," meaning: I have heard something nice about you, but I'll only tell "last" after you've told me a compliment you've heard about me. Rena explained all this to me, and both she and Ruth would challenge me to match them with a T. L. Promissory notes were not accepted. One had to come up with an exchange promptly. Finding myself caught short, I would hurry into the kitchen. "Mama, please say something nice about Rena."

Aware of the stakes, she would pause, look up from the pot on the stove and thoughtfully brush back a strand of hair. "Well now . . . Rena has an infectious laugh."

With such a tidbit to offer, I could learn, for instance,

that one of Rena's friends had said her little brother was cute. Thus we salved the wounded vanities that go with growing up.

At times, gathered in the dining room in the evening, our family resembled the bucolic communion of Whittier's "Snow-bound." But a truer recollection shows individuals meeting a variety of outside schedules. Being on time was important—for school and church, and even more for the men's jobs. My sisters had many after-school activities, went on dates, and attended interschool competitions in other towns. Institutions outside the family attracted us and coerced us. Did we want it any other way? Even my mother, the most homebound, kept imagining great futures for her children in a limitless America.

CHAPTER 8

Where I Wandered

Locust, elm, poplar, and evergreen trees shade the one-and-one-half acre Goodland City Park, which has a fountain and wading pool in its center.

—*The WPA Guide to 1930s Kansas*, p. 335

FREEDOM to go out to play stayed much the same after the move to Goodland. The main rule, one I'd learned early back in Herington, remained: look both ways before crossing the street. Instructions about how far away to go and when to come home proved no barriers to visiting classmates and exploring the town.

In Herington I had little reason to seek playmates beyond our long block on C Street. No other children lived in our block on Walnut Street, and I had to walk a ways to find a companion. Rather than making any prearrangement, I usually simply strolled by houses I knew to see if my friends were outdoors.

Even if I found no one to play with, I enjoyed myself, looking at the designs of people's front doors, noticing where trees were bigger than the two I watered, seeing how the school looked with nobody about. Often my gaze was downward, at the tilt of broken sidewalk, the scrubbiness of roadside grass, the inscriptions on discarded candy wrappers. Perhaps I would meet someone I knew who could play, or join up with a new comrade. I didn't feel lonely if I encountered no one.

One day I took along Dean's old box Kodak, our only camera, long out of use. Unsure whether it contained film, but hoping it did, I spent much of the morning snapping pictures not of people, but of houses, cars in garages, and smaller objects—pebbles and even odd-shaped cracks in the sidewalk. I began to suspect that my enthusiasm had exceeded the capacity of any possible roll of film. Of course the camera contained none.

Two or three streets away I could find the homes of classmates. Some lived east of Walnut Street, where the town frazzled out, with sometimes only a single house to a block. My most frequent pal, whose parents had ebulliently named him Joy, lived on the very edge of town in a "basement house." I never heard my family disparage this domicile. In fact, discussions emphasized its cleverness, warm in winter and cool in summer. In better times one could of course build on top of the basement.

Mostly the two of us played outside, but the one time Joy's smiling mother invited us to come in, I found glasses of lemonade waiting on the oilcloth-covered table. It was indeed cool inside, and cozy. Usually Joy came by my house. With an apologetic grin he would knock on the kitchen door, finding more often than not that yes, Hugh could come out and play.

Sometimes we did nothing more exciting than pulling the heads off the all-too-available grasshoppers, trying to complete the decapitation before they could spit tobacco juice on us. It was more fun, if the workers had left, to investigate the bricks and lumber assembled for the new high school under construction across the street from the Fowler house. Later, with the building completed, the new agriculture teacher, Mr. Whipps, and his students bred turkeys behind the school. We pelted them with sticks to

A new high school rose across from the Fowler house. Piles of construction material provided me a temporary playground. Courtesy of Parker Collection, Sherman County Historical Society.

see if they would fly. As far as we could observe, they didn't know how.

In the sparsely settled area beyond Walnut Street, the Amos house, with its faded paint, jutted out of a barren yard, probably not three stories high, though that is how I remember it. Beverly Amos lived there, the skinniest girl in my class and a good friend, who often walked home from school with me. Her two brothers were older, but once when she wasn't around, I spent the afternoon with them.

The brothers' latest project had been to dig a cave in the vacant lot next door. Their labor impressed me, but I hesitated to descend into anything so deep and smelly. Their invitation, more of a challenge, proved irresistible. The hole dropped well beyond my height, but I let myself down and crawled through the sharp bend into the part of the cave that ran parallel to the surface. After a gruesome pause, I backed out and let myself be helped out of the entrance hole. I assured the Amos boys that of course I had crawled to the very end. They seemed to believe me and even helped brush off the dirt that might betray this risky exploit when I got home.

Although the Amos boys showed no interest in attending the play I authored for presentation in our basement, their three sisters formed the bulk of the audience. The theme and any collaborators have faded from memory. Though perhaps not quite. I refuse to follow the wisp of memory that suggests "You must pay the rent!" as one bit of dialogue.

Rena or Ruth must have helped me adapt the old bedsheet that served as a stage curtain. I pulled it open and shut and also starred in the one-act drama. With modest expectations, I had distributed a few handwritten flyers about the performance and was much relieved when the Amos sisters appeared.

Standing at the basement door I held every entrant to the full two-cent admission charge announced in the flyer. One of the Amos girls had to pay with her Indian-head pennies, coins treasured almost mystically by grade-schoolers. Since these were worth more than the Lincoln heads, I felt a little guilty. I kept them for a long time, a persisting reminder of my theatrical venture and my mercenary effort to market my talent.

Convenient though it was that Joy and the Amos kids lived in our part of town, I felt no need to limit companionship to them. It hardly mattered that Lyle lived halfway across town. Often both his parents were away, and although they hired an older woman to take care of him, we easily ignored her complaints as we banged about his basement.

Down the street from Lyle's stood one of the oldest houses in town, a two-story with dark paint and heavily curtained windows. In its front room the widow who lived there ran a small candy and notions shop. Years later when I read *The House of the Seven Gables*, the aura of this house enlivened the setting. We found the owner scary in her long black dress and oval spectacles, but we knew a bargain when we saw one. Her ice-cream cones—I admit, smaller than most—sold at two for a nickel.

Anyone in my room at school I considered a friend, and intimacy came easily. Beverly Amos's cousin Audrey, also in our class, didn't look at all like her, being short and dark-haired. Audrey lived far from Walnut Street, in quarters behind her father's small grocery, what would later be called a mom-and-pop store. I visited her there only once, perhaps by invitation or perhaps I was out strolling and just turned up. Her parents welcomed me, and we played in front of the store on the broad Main Street sidewalk and in the living room at the rear.

Audrey had a trove of comic books, all with the covers torn off. I knew little about these gaudy magazines, though I liked the daily comics. Her parents agreed that she could give me some, but warned me to conceal them. They had been a gift from the unsold supply at the newsstand run by the old man next door. I took the conspiracy to heart, holding the plunder awkwardly under my shirt. Audrey walked me halfway home. After a few blocks she laughed at my bent-over posture. "You can take them out now," she said. "We only meant not to show them while we walked by Mr. Mack's stand." Back home no one paid any attention to my acquisition. I'm sure I read every page, but that went quickly and gave no great satisfaction. In those pre-Superman days, the comic books did not addict me.

It did make a difference if a girl was pretty, though she mustn't be stuck-up about it. One friend reported with horror that a younger child, hearing someone praised by adults as pretty, had shamelessly announced: "I'm pretty too!" This "tooting one's own horn" (Rena's phrase) was contemptible. With her large eyes and dimples Ardith Ann Tilly had no need to praise her looks, and anyway she was too sweet to brag. Again and again I strolled by her house hoping she would be outdoors. When that was the case, I looked no further for someone to play with. If she intended to play jacks, I observed with admiration. If she had chalked a hopscotch track on the sidewalk, we both participated, and it didn't trouble me that she showed greater skill.

Out of the general affection I extended to all my classmates, one other ten-year-old emerged as my "girlfriend," much to my surprise. One day as she saw me sauntering by her house, Thelma Wilson jumped off her bicycle, a boy's bicycle handed down by her brother, and we exchanged a little news of classmates' doings. Then with an intense, serious look, she asked me, "Do you like a particular girl as a girlfriend?" I gave the safest answer, and the truthful one, "Not really." That seemed abrupt, so I added, "Do you have a boyfriend?"

"Yes I do. And it's you."

I shivered with gratitude. I told her that indeed I did think of her in that special way. It felt good to be chosen, and from then on Thelma's house was the first place I went to look for companionship.

I had always liked Thelma, whose older sister was one of Rena's best friends. Thelma's freckles and straight hair made her anything but a Shirley Temple look-alike. Her homemade dresses lacked the crisp prettiness of Ardith Ann's wardrobe. I thought of Thelma as something of a tomboy, and playing with her took lots of energy. None of this mattered.

Did anything physical follow this rush of reciprocal affection? Neither of us offered the other kisses, but Thelma did ride me on her bicycle. Sitting between her arms on the crossbar as she pumped along, I inhaled a comforting mix of breath and sweat.

She invited me for supper one day, and we spent the evening using my new printing set to issue a newspaper. "What should we name it?" she asked. I was embarrassed to have no idea, but I spotted a dime-store print of Cupid on the Wilsons' living room wall. "Why not call it *The Cupid*?" Having nothing better in mind, Thelma agreed. We intended no claim that the arrows of love had struck us, a meaning Dean later pretended to discern.

The economic circumstances of Thelma's family raised no barrier to our special bond. I knew that her father worked for the WPA, not as good a situation as working for the Rock Island. But why should I care? At the supper table he sat shrunken and taciturn, his wife cheerily managing everything. The meal consisted principally of bread and bologna, each slice of meat rolled separately to fill the serving plate. Though urged to take more, I held back and left the table still hungry.

Still, it was a grand evening, with *The Cupid* as a triumph to display back home. In the fifth grade, dates were unimagined, but Thelma remained special. On my only return visit to Goodland, in 1944, it was she who welcomed me and took me around to see former teachers and our now teen-aged classmates.

Sometimes I wandered as far as the town's only park, a square of grass and trees that lay far from the Fowler house, several blocks the other side of Main Street. My parents had no objections when I occasionally announced the park as my destination. Probably they thought that this bit of nature made a healthy environment.

Fronting the park, a steep-roofed brick edifice formed the center of a cluster of buildings. I could glimpse a small flower garden through one of the archways in the surrounding wall, and the general appearance reminded me of castles pictured in *The Book of Knowledge*. The fact that this was "the Catholic church," though known to me, had only faint connotations. Any church other than ours seemed exotic, but the beauty and extensiveness of this one drew special attention.

On a certain day, when I had teamed up with a slightly younger boy also at loose ends in the park, we grew bored with its limited amusements. Let's go explore that church, I suggested. He hung back a little. I assured him that all churches were supposed to be open, and since it wasn't Sunday, nobody would be there anyway.

Expecting some inner grandeur to match the alluring exterior, we crossed the street, admired the garden close up, and entered through what we took to be the back door. We proceeded undeterred, even attracted, by a mysteriously sweet odor. The door at the end of the hall led us not into the sanctuary, but into a small carpeted study. There in a leather chair, dressed in black with a book open on his knees, sat a youngish man who looked up at us with a blend of mild surprise and reassurance, raised eyebrows, and a gently inquiring smile.

Far from reassured, we fled, down the hall, through the garden, and beyond the park, which now seemed perilously close to the scene of our crime. We had meant no harm, I told myself, preparing a defense in case of capture. We had only been exploring and appreciating.

"Where did you play today?"

"Nobody was home at the Wilsons', and I played in the park with a friend." There was no need to tell about the trespass and narrow escape.

Fear made the church invasion memorable. Shame gave permanence to the recollection of another far-across-town misadventure. Even farther away from our house than the town park, the fairgrounds usually sat deserted, its steep wooden bleachers, which we called the grandstand, flanked by a few open sheds. The area had looked far different when the fair was in progress. Still, the very barrenness of the ground and vacancy of the structures invited exploration.

I found myself out there one day, a little lonely, happy to see three boys racing up and down the grandstand. Though I didn't know them, I joined in the exercise. After a bit, we stopped to catch our breath at the topmost row and exchanged some guarded get-acquainted comments.

They showed me a treasure they had discovered in the trash under the plank seats, an empty Prince Albert tobacco can on which someone had scratched out certain letters from the description printed on the back. It now read not of the excellence of Prince Albert tobacco, but: "Pa covered Ma to produce Pat and me." Not much impressed by this piece of folk art, I tried to be positive, agreeing with them that this was a great find.

Still, my friendliness was not winning approval from these chance companions. Perhaps I had been clumsy racing up the bleacher steps. Perhaps I was the only one not in overalls. Perhaps my response to the Prince Albert revision had seemed halfhearted, or they simply wanted to tighten their own bond by labeling an outsider. Abruptly, with no connection to our talk that I could see, one asked me, "Are you a sissy?"

I wanted to keep playing with these boys. I wanted their approval. Defensively, I answered with a comment I had once heard my mother make about me: "I've been sick a lot."

They hooted and bounded away. I realized at once that this had been a shoddy appeal. Probably it wasn't even true. I shoved my hands in my pockets and headed home, disappointed in myself and vowing never to say that again.

CHAPTER 9

When the Family Traveled

The foreign passes are here.

—My father

M Y PARENTS determined early on to show their children that small Midwestern towns did not constitute the world. Often family conversation centered on yet another trip, it being understood that railroad transportation came free, an occupational benefit in which Dad took great pride.

In old age he would introduce himself to strangers as having worked fifty-two years on the Rock Island (or, when memory played him false, the Santa Fe, his first railroad employer, before he left Emporia). Encouraged in his eighties to set down his life story, he wrote at length about the trip he had taken with his two older children in 1924, visiting relatives along the West Coast, all accomplished with his "foreign passes." This reciprocal right of railroad employees to travel gratis on other companies' lines took considerable planning, form-completion skill, and patience. Dad provided all of these. After much suspense, and sometimes at the last moment, he would nonchalantly announce that the foreign passes had come.

The longest trip of the Goodland years took my mother and my three sisters to Southern California. As an officer in the Quill, a student writing society, Helene wanted to participate in its national convention scheduled for Pasadena, and there was no good reason to limit the foreign pass to one person. As plans matured, it remained unclear whether or not I would go along, and I came to count on going. I found train rides fun and of course wanted to see the place the movies came from. Practical considerations indicated that four women could have a much more convenient trip if not accompanied by a seven-year-old boy, yet if left behind I would be deeply disappointed.

Uncharacteristically for our family, where children had duties and were not to be bribed, I was offered a reward if I would stay home with Dad and Dean. "The girls" would leave presents for me, and I could have one each day. These new acquisitions went a long way to salving my hurt feelings. If not quite a bonanza, the gifts provided a daily high point. On the new board game, decorated with college pennants, a small brass football could be moved up and down a simulated gridiron. Each move depended on the result of a spun dial and the previous choice of whether to kick, pass, run, or plunge. I could at least imagine myself in the role of the pictured cheerleaders, both male. Other gifts included a yo-yo, which I never quite mastered, and the card game Authors, which Dean indulgently played with me. Just who Sir Walter Scott was didn't matter, but getting all four cards with his picture did.

Dad had insisted that it would be great fun for the three males in the family to "batch." Both he and Dean could cook, and I suffered no dietary deprivation. I didn't much like Dad's fried mush, but Dean declared I should be proud to eat it, since our ancestors had lived for days off that and molasses. On the cement sidewalk behind the Kimmel house, Dean taught me a game he had invented of imagined auto trips. We would pick a nearby town, use a roadmap to figure its distance from Goodland, and then bounce a golf ball the required number of times, one bounce per mile. Failure to catch the ball meant "change drivers."

Frequent postcards from the womenfolk told of their "wonderful time," and details followed on their return. Helene had had her picture taken with Hamlin Garland, allegedly a major American author. They had toured a movie lot and attended a live drama at the Pasadena Playhouse. After her wider travels, Rena displayed an irritating superiority, but I was so glad to have everybody back that I put up with her.

In competition with the Union Pacific and the Santa Fe, the Rock Island served Topeka, where it had its own gray Gothic station. Accordingly, we traveled there from Goodland on the standard Rock Island pass. On overnight trips we usually took the Pullman sleeper, where pass holders could get half-rate. Sleeping in an upper berth with an adult was an adventure in contortion, but the clicking wheels helped me fall asleep. We encountered dark-skinned, uniformed men when we took the Pullman, porters who impressively combined officiousness with polished manners. They made up our berths with panache, and their brushing of ladies' and gentlemen's coats as they left the train elicited a quarter or even more from my parsimonious parents.

Changing trains in McFarland allowed time for a snack in the vast dining room of the Modoc Hotel. Its huge circular counter and lack of booths revealed a design for rapid serving of railroad passengers in long-ago boom times. Given the exploitative prices, we ate sparingly. Besides, we had packed a lunch to consume on the train.

Topeka visits came so frequently that three male cousins there became my good buddies, and, since they lived on farms, I learned a lot about the seasonal pace of agricultural work and some enlightening details about livestock anatomy. "Hughie, what do you think that big red thing under the bull's belly is?" Don asked me with a nudge. When by chance I overheard adult conversations, they treated the drought (pronounced "drouth"), the inadequacy of government aid programs, and the greed of the middleman. I disliked the complaining tone of it all, but I did relish some new words and admire my parents' ease in using them, words like "silage," "harrowing," and the passionately uttered "parity."

It was especially important not to miss the major Eddy family reunion, always on the Fourth of July. It took place at Indian Hill Farm, where in keeping with the name one cousin kept finding stone arrowheads for his collection. Mother had grown up there, and now her brother Harry operated it. The size of the gathering overwhelmed me. Distant cousins appeared out of nowhere, some startlingly rustic in dress and speech. To bring the hubbub under control, Aunt Lois led us in singing "The More We Get Together" ("the happier we'll be"). We stayed quiet then as Grandmother "returned thanks." Her voice carried well, and she asked grace a bit more briefly on these occasions, though never omitting the request that God "finally own us in heaven."

Everybody brought food, and everything tasted good. The children sat at a separate table, pampered by a variety of aunts and given more food than was good for us. I ate so many deviled eggs that I could not do justice to the fried chicken. The watermelons came out of big washtubs full of ice, and the men spelled each other in turning the crank to prepare the homemade ice cream.

As evening set in, I joined my cousins in catching lightening bugs. If you crushed one just as it flickered on, you had the makings of a fine glowing finger ring.

We saw less of my father's family, in Emporia, and I found visits there somewhat tense. The big brown house on Congress Street awed me with its shadowy front hall and huge framed photographs of relatives in World War I uniforms. Three of Grandmother Hawkins's children still lived there with her, unmarried Uncle Cliff and Aunt Kit as well as Aunt Grace, whose husband, Luther, had died early in their marriage. Aunt Kit enjoyed reminding the family that Grace deserved special treatment, given the biblical command to care for ministers' widows.

Emporia provided cousins close in age to each of us five siblings. I paired off with Frederick, Uncle Jonas and Aunt Ella's son. His husky frame foretold his future as an Albuquerque policeman, but he did lead me into mischief. One rainy day he showed me Grandmother's backstairs, and we mounted them all the way up to her attic. Orienting ourselves after a little sneezing, we pushed aside disused lamps and broken chairs to reach a mysterious trunk. It opened with a rusty protest, but yielded, besides some uninteresting rolls of fabric, Aunt Grace's girlhood report cards. In the murky light we marveled at the antiquated course names, marking system, and handwriting. Deciding she must have been a model student, we carefully closed the trunk.

After we descended, Aunt Kit cornered us and asked for assurance that we had not intruded into any of her sister's precious things. We lied.

Since none of his children were my age, I saw little of my father's older brother Earl, but I did absorb the family pride in his having been mayor of Emporia and in his residence, directly across the street from William Allen White, editor of the *Emporia Gazette*. Since White's article about his daughter's fatal riding accident appeared in the book for Rena's English class, I decided he, like Hamlin Garland, must be a famous writer. Disconcertingly, White had written editorials against my uncle's candidacy in 1923. Which was more important, approval by a renowned editor or victory at the polls? Only in the 1940s, when White's autobiography appeared, did I learn that the Ku Klux Klan's support for my uncle had inspired the editor's opposition.

When I asked if this terrible charge could be true, Dad confirmed it. "Yes, accepting Klan support was a bad mistake." A budding teenage liberal, I would have been happier with this evaluation if Dad hadn't added, "He could have won easily without it."

Mother overheard the exchange, and a rare quarrel between my parents followed. Dad insisted that one of Mother's brothers had been a Klansman, a claim she dismissed as impossible. "Well, he did take me along to one of their meetings," Dad offered, and the matter was dropped. The exchange left me even more curious about this world that had so closely preceded my own birth.

After buying the Chrysler in 1936, my parents began to think of the car as the most convenient, though not the least expensive, transportation for vacation trips. States to the west of Goodland beckoned with well-advertised destinations, some of them unreachable by rail. Our trips west gave me a sense of space very different from the rolling landscape near Topeka or the uninterrupted tableland around Goodland. Now I experienced the thrill of steep upgrades that threatened to overheat the car's engine, and sheer drop-offs that made me imagine the car sliding over the edge, tumbling down and down. On Colorado highways small signs with skulls (or was it crosses?) indicated the number of traffic deaths at certain spots. By all this I was more exhilarated than frightened.

As we crested some foothills and paused before starting down into a wide valley, I exclaimed, "Look at all that territory!" General hilarity in response. Not that I minded the attention, but I didn't see what was funny. Later in private I asked Mother, who was a good explainer, why folks had laughed. After brief reflection she said, "I suppose it was such a big word for a little boy." This comment of course did nothing to discourage my absorption of adult vocabulary as I sat enthralled by grown-ups' talk.

One Colorado trip included La Junta, where my father's Uncle Jim and his wife, Cora, ran a boarding house. This struck me as an exciting way of life, and the many bedrooms gave us luxuriously spacious sleeping quarters. Learning that they had had ten children, most of them now grown and away, I concluded that family size explained the original purchase of so large a house. The managerial drive seemed predominantly that of Aunt Cora, whose jolly self-possession I found irresistible. "Instead of Great-aunt Cora," I told her, "I'm going to call you dear Aunt Cora." She rewarded me with a hug.

All happy memories? Not quite. At the La Junta boarding house occurred one of the most frightening experiences of my life. Sleeping in the same vast room as my parents, I had awakened first. From my cot near the open, unscreened window, I gazed out at the early sunlight. The leaves on the ivy that encroached on the window began to tremble a little, though there was no wind. Then a snake, plump, brown, and sinuous, slipped along the sill. It didn't try to come into the room, but I was still terrified. Would it enter some other room and bite somebody? Should I wake my parents and warn them? Would any mention of the snake embarrass Aunt Cora? Would they say I was just dreaming? I decided to say nothing about the creature, but over the years, leaf-edged windows have evoked this childhood dread.

The car took us to two wonders of the West. Our visits to Yellowstone Park and to Carlsbad Caverns differed little from what thousands of our contemporaries could recall with the help of their preserved picture postcards. As distinctly as waiting for Old Faithful, I remember the wonder inspired by the sign in one Wyoming town declaring it the home of the original JCPenney, a surprising contradiction to the familiar charge that all the big chains came from "back East." More memorable than the Yellowstone bears was the owner of a Montana guesthouse near the park, a rangy, no-nonsense woman who, after our night's sleep, led us halfway up the mountain in her backyard to share her favorite view.

The National Park Service guides at Carlsbad Caverns gave a tour that included sympathetic descriptions of bats' behavior as well as the experience of total darkness, impossible to obtain on the earth's surface. For a long time we remembered the difference between stalactites and stalagmites; it escapes me now. The guide's instruction to touch nothing, since clean though your hands might be, they still left a stain, survived as a staple in Mother's cautionary advice.

So close to Mexico in Carlsbad, why not cross the border for an international experience? After a night in El Paso, with Ruth at the wheel, we drove to the Rio Grande. Before we could get on the bridge, an official-looking fellow with an emblazoned cap motioned us to the side. Ruth didn't want to oblige him, but my parents insisted she pull over. The man was in fact a taxi driver urging the advantages of leaving our car and crossing in his taxi for a tour under his guidance. He made a good case, and we piled in, soon admiring his control of the bustling streets in Ciudad Juarez.

He took us to the arena and verbally re-created a bullfight. Mildly horrified, we still laughed at his jokes about the cheaper seats with no shade and the refusal of locals to buy beef the day after a bullfight. At a souvenir shop, whose owner seemed the taxi driver's close acquaintance if not a relative, Mother selected a few items, notably a large tray made from a gourd bottom, bright red with incised animal figures in black. Back home it hung incongruously amid our somber dining-room furniture.

As a final demonstration of his prowess, the driver hardly paused at the U.S. border station. "All Americans," he announced and swept us back to our own waiting car.

On one of these trips, the family drove by a camp of the Civilian Conservation Corps. Someone in the car declared that "the CCC" was a good way for the government to help "poor boys." I glimpsed stark barracks and a few young men in ugly uniforms, but I felt sure they were escaping something worse, like the life of hobos, whose trash I had seen when exploring empty boxcars near the depot.

Salt Lake City came unexpectedly as a spur-of-the-moment extension of a Colorado trip. The lake itself looked uninviting, though I had wanted to test the claim that one floated there with ease. A visit to the Mormon Tabernacle filled our morning. Under supervision of the Mormon guide, as engaging as the National Park staff, we heard the drop of a pin that proved the excellence of the tabernacle's acoustics, and we accepted his explanation of why non-Mormons were not allowed in the nearby Temple. In the gift shop, Mother paid the small amount requested for *The Book of Mormon*, telling us it would be of historical interest. None of us ever read it, of course.

A favorite cousin of Dad's, Clark Hetherington, lived with his family in Galveston, and, after some years of invitations, we made the trip there by train, probably in 1939. The railroad passed through Oklahoma City's shantytown. The close-packed accumulation of jerry-built shacks appalled us, and I was glad when the train left them behind. We speculated that nothing similar existed in our native Kansas.

The trip provided my first sight of any coast and a chance to observe ocean tides. The Hetheringtons showed us the seawall and told us tales of the great hurricane of 1900. We watched banana boats being unloaded. Sometimes, Clark told us, tarantulas sprang out of the huge bunches. When one longshoreman pocketed some yellow bananas after breaking them off a comrade's load, I was assured this was not theft. Those bananas would have been overripe before reaching the market.

Best of all, the son, Johnny, three years older than I was, proved a great pal. My name stirred his interest. "The only other person I ever heard of with that name is Huey Long." Everybody but me knew who Huey Long was. I didn't mind that an eminent personage shared my name, but it was irritating to find people favoring his spelling over my "Hughie."

During the three days we were in Galveston Johnny taught me the needed balance to ride a bicycle, though I didn't quite master the art of starting off or stopping without help. Even better, we practiced wrestling before we fell asleep, and he declared me a good wrestler.

From every trip, whether we visited relatives or natural wonders, we returned home happily. We had missed the familiar objects and daily routines of Goodland. Yet as our horizons broadened, it was hard to believe that any of us would live out our lives there.

CHAPTER 10

Changed Lives

Do you know what's going on?

—My mother

BEFORE I was born, and before I could understand their significance, our family history had of course included important developments, not least the births of children and the vicissitudes of my father's railroad career. For me, however, the changes that left Rena and me as the only children at home in 1939 and the move in 1940 to another town in another state revealed a world full of surprises, even of marvels, of possibilities and losses.

Only one of these changes made me cry—Helene's marriage. She had been away at college for most of the time that I could remember, but that had not kept her from being a strong presence in the family. To her younger siblings she represented the richness life could offer. When she came home on vacations, she brought some of the paraphernalia of college life—the yearbook, her sorority pin, a scarf with school colors. Her challenges to the judgments of my parents succeeded far better than the occasional rebellions of Ruth or Rena. One summer Helene worked at the YMCA camp at Estes Park, Colorado. Our visit there found her in a spectacular Rocky Mountain setting with many new friends and hilarious tales about some of the guests.

I suspected that I was her favorite. She was fifteen when I was born. My mother liked to have her older children take care of the younger, and perhaps Helene could draw on nascent maternal instincts. I sometimes thought of her as a second mother. Once on a train trip that she and I made together, she played along when I suggested that we pretend she was my mother to see if we could fool the other passengers. We rather overdid it, every sentence ending with "Mother" or "Son," but I felt sure we had been convincing.

Although Helene majored in history and political science and minored in journalism, she took many physical education courses. In her last year at Washburn she began working part-time as a recreational therapist at the world-famous Menninger Clinic in Topeka, a pioneer in psychiatric medicine. She joked that all she had to do was "play tennis with the patients." In fact, however, she became a valued staff member and a friend of the Menningers, working full-time after her graduation. We still saw her often, Topeka being the family's most frequent travel destination.

Always there had been boyfriends, but she was—or so we understood—engaged to Bud Van Zandt, a young engineer who had graduated from Washburn a few years earlier. He visited us in Goodland and took special pains to befriend me, even sent presents, and I counted on having this tall blond fellow as my brother-in-law. It was all settled as far as I was concerned.

Helene's letters home weren't shared with me, but I heard intimations that the love match wasn't going well. In an automobile accident, with Bud at the wheel, Helene had broken the windshield with the back of her head. Luckily, she hadn't been facing forward. Hardly an engagement-breaking incident, though Mother once implied as much. More significantly, as I heard later, Bud maintained that no wife of his was going to work.

Helene with Dr. Morse. She was a June bride—barely. They married on June 30, 1938, in the garden of the Menninger Clinic. Author's collection.

I began to hear veiled comments about "the doctor," and snapshots arrived showing a quizzical-looking, mustached fellow, whose best feature was his eyes, focused lovingly on Helene. In the spring of 1938, Mother asked, "Do you know what's going on?"

"Yes,—that!" I said, pointing to one of the photographs and bursting into tears. It was bad enough losing Helene to a husband, but for her not to bring Bud Van Zandt into the family made it catastrophic.

As we joked later, she barely made it as a June bride. The wedding, June 30, 1938, took place in the rock garden of the Clinic. An informal affair, it included some instrumental music, but only one attendant each for bride and groom. My father did not accompany Helene to the makeshift altar, and the minister did not ask who gave her in marriage. Our family sat together, thinking her very beautiful in the dress carefully chosen so that it could serve later as an evening gown.

My tears afterward brought lots of gentle attention from some of Helene's nurse friends. "I cried too," Rena told me, "but nobody noticed."

Ruth's departure for college in September 1939 did not seem as sharp a break. Rena and I shared the sense of adventure as Ruth examined the brochures from Colorado Women's College. In our eyes its exclusive admission of women gave it an aura of gentility, and Denver fit our ideal of a sophisticated, prosperous city. Just as I had yearned to be old enough to enter first grade, I began anticipating the stimulation and independence of going away to college.

Mother read Ruth's letters aloud as soon as they arrived. She described positively her voice training and her speech class. The president knew every student by name. I took special interest in her new friends, one of whom came from a ranch in Wyoming with genuine cowboys. Ruth passed on to us her friend's scorn for the way movie cowboys wore their neckerchiefs—far too loose to serve their true purpose, keeping the dirt out of the cowpuncher's neck. Ruth's roommate hoped to become a mortician. "That's fine," Ruth wrote, "as long as she doesn't wake up some night and decide to go to work."

A photograph of her room showed Ruth smiling, cross-legged on her bed, with matching counterpane and draperies that she had selected herself in a Denver department store.

Good news flowed in. Besides her acceptance as a member of the choir at the Episcopal Church, a paying job, word came that she was dating a young member of that church. To mention his family's name in Denver, she confided, was "really saying something." She regularly visited the home of my father's most successful cousin, Willy Schofield, a Denver attorney, whose wife, also named Ruth, was, even though she smoked, "a lovely person."

Saddened though I was by Helene's move to faraway

Maryland, she had not been a daily member of the family circle for several years. With Dean it was different. He had always been there. Although his adult interests set him somewhat apart, he usually drove on our family outings, and he would make sure we had a light supper if my mother, worn out from preparing Sunday dinner, lost interest in the kitchen. Sometimes we slept together, and he taught me to "sleep spoons," explaining that any other posture meant my kicks would keep him awake all night.

Why Dean moved out in the fall of 1939 remained unclear to me. Others in the family seemed to approve, and I saw no evidence of animosity. Earlier, I had overheard Mother refer to his beginning to pay something toward family expenses, now that "we have these extra burdens" (possibly the costs of Ruth's going to college). Did he decide he might as well pay rent elsewhere? I can recall Ruth's declaring to a friend that this move would be good for Dean and that, though his new landlady was a prune, he could if necessary evade her curfew by climbing in and out through a window.

It didn't occur to me at the time, but for a twenty-eight-year-old, even mild parental oversight had to be galling. The folks continued all too conscientiously to give advice to their adult children, as each of the five could ultimately testify. In Dean's case, his spell of mental illness along with occasional ulcer attacks led my parents to treat him somewhat as an invalid.

Demographic studies show that in the Depression decade children stayed with parents late into their adult years, and marriages were delayed. Dean didn't have these statistics and didn't think about broad social forces, but by the time he moved out he was surely impatient to be more than son and brother.

He wasn't unemployed, after all. He was the book-keeper, in fact the entire office force, at the O. K. Packing

Behind the Fowler house, by the goldfish pond, Mother, Dean, and Dad stand close together in the winter wind. Author's collection.

Company, located just out of town in a cinder-block building fronted by steep steps leading up to the office. Remembering the stench of slaughter, I dreaded going along in the car on days when we picked Dean up after work, but it always pleased me to see him come out the door cheery and confident.

Dean became friends with the chief butcher, who felt exploited by the owner and wanted to strike out for himself, though lacking knowledge of the paperwork side of the business. Dean agreed to go in with him, contributing some of his savings. Together they would buy an available butchering plant in Atwood, some sixty miles northeast of Goodland, near the Nebraska border. What fun to name one's own business, I thought, when Dean explained that they had picked the name R Square Packing Company. But perhaps the "square" in Teddy Roosevelt's Square Deal had lost resonance during FDR's New Deal. As it turned out, local people misread the emblem put in ads and on meat packages. They saw the R in a square, not as a promise to deal fairly, but as an effort to honor Rawlins, the name of the county.

Strong advocates of saving, the folks had encouraged Dean to put money into Investors Diversified Services, the Minneapolis firm in which my father had great faith. For Dean to risk his financial reserves on an independent business venture seemed foolhardy, given the long record of Depression bankruptcies. I recall only Dean's positive description of the plan, but almost certainly my parents warned against it.

Another change in Dean's life closely followed this business decision. We all knew that Faye was his girlfriend, but out of my hearing, he had probably been warned against marriage, given his health and the condition of the economy. Or perhaps such caution had simply been the implication of family talk over the years. His sardonic misogyny

Dean and Faye, shortly after my favorite Sunday school teacher became my sister-in-law. Author's collection.

had seemed a guarantee of continued bachelorhood. But Dean, it turned out, was now a new man.

Toward noon one day, as Mother, Rena, and I sat in the kitchen eating lunch, Dean and Faye entered through the back door. "Mother, meet your new daughter-in-law." Mother's response of "Oh, no!" was hardly reassuring.

"Yes, this morning," Faye chimed in, extending her left hand with its new diamond ring.

As they prepared to leave, Mother instructed Dean to come back so that she could have a word with him. Rena and I were ordered out of the kitchen. Now, if ever, we felt like comrades. Banished with me to a bedroom, my red-faced sister muttered through gritted teeth, "That woman!" A little scared by this sudden turmoil, I tried to sympathize. But I soon remembered that I liked Faye and her family. Elopement—if that's what had happened—struck me as something out of a very good movie. This sister-in-law promised to be a nice addition to the family, quite different from the incursion of an unknown brother-in-law.

Weeks later I overheard Mother explaining what she had said to Dean. She had warned him to take care that Faye, being so young, did not get pregnant. Not one of Mother's more insightful moments.

How We Left Goodland and Saw the World of Tomorrow

Today as the Fair is rushed to a frantic completion, it can
safely be said that it will be exciting, impressive and
eminently worthwhile.

—*Life*, March 13, 1939, p. 33

PERHAPS because he foresaw further consolidations by
the Rock Island, my father never had us buy a house in
Goodland. Perhaps I was not the only one hoping to
return somehow to beloved Herington with its hills and
tall trees. By 1939 the news had come: the Goodland
dispatchers' office would close. Since Dad's seniority dated
from 1904, he could "bid in" to another office pretty much
as he chose. He could "bump" any dispatcher with less seniority and take his place.

Possibilities included Fairbury, Nebraska, and Dalhart,
Texas. When the Goodland office went the way of the Herington office, he worked briefly in each, and the family visited him to consider these towns as new homes. I recall my
dismay at the possibility of moving to Nebraska. Since no
movies were ever set there, it lacked the status of Kansas,
confirmed by both *The Wizard of Oz* and *Dodge City*.
Misunderstanding my complaint, Mother tried to reassure
me that certain movie stars had indeed been born in
Nebraska, but that of course missed the point.

Dad's ultimate choice of El Reno, Oklahoma, was carefully reasoned. Since it was a division point on the Rock Island where east-west and north-south lines crossed, the dispatchers' office there could never be abolished. At age fifty-two he was tired of moving. Although we did not know the town, El Reno appealed to us. Its Spanish name suggested an exotic Mexican flavor. Nearby Oklahoma City, despite its shantytown, would offer some of the urban attractions of Denver. The presence of the recently founded El Reno Junior College meant that Ruth could live at home for her second year of college, then shift to the University of Oklahoma in Norman, so close it could be reached by the interurban trolley. And doubtless in a southern state winters would be less severe.

Before Dad took up his new post, since he had never seen portions of the lines he would control, he took trips with freight-train crews, living with them in the caboose. I could hardly imagine a more exciting adventure. About this time Dad gained a vividness for me that makes it much easier to recall his words and actions. Had something given him a new assertiveness, or was I simply maturing in a way that increased my interest in how a man behaved?

In certain ways we were sorry to leave Goodland. I parted from good friends and regretted never being able to attend the new high school with so many teachers whom the family admired. We would live farther away from Dean, but he had begun a separate life. I recall no complaints from Ruth about not returning to Colorado Women's College. She had already stopped seeing her Denver boyfriend. She wrote the institution's president a letter, explaining why she would not return but praising her unforgettable first college year. A letter wishing her well soon arrived, signed, to her delight, "Prexy."

But for Rena the break, midway through high school, came hard. Rather lonely in the new town that first sum-

*We admired the El Reno depot, which we found rather exotic.
Courtesy of the Canadian County Historical Museum.*

mer, she spent hours composing careful letters to her clos-
est Goodland friends and seemed almost to welcome my
company.

In May 1940 the move got underway. Dad used his
employee's privileges to reserve free use of a boxcar. We
loaded in our furniture and even the new Buick, which Mr.
Griest, who knew all about cars, helped to block in and tie
down. Even so, the boxcar's vast interior remained half
empty.

We reached El Reno by train, making a brief stopover in
Topeka on the way, sharing our anticipations with the relatives there. With what seemed to me lavish expenditure,
we lived for a few days after our arrival in rooms at a guesthouse and ate in restaurants. Surveying the local attractions, we discovered beautiful churches, mostly brick or
stone, at least one pillared residence that fit our idea of a
southern mansion, and a railroad station far more spacious

than Goodland's. The Rock Island office building where Dad worked, an imposing brick three-story on West Watts, ranked among the biggest buildings in town. All this, plus three movie theaters.

Free swimming lessons at the new WPA-constructed municipal pool provided a way to meet other youngsters before school started. In line waiting for admission the first day, one boy found a small card reading, "Free Sample." He thrust it into the hand of a girl standing nearby, commenting jauntily, "I'll give you a free sample!" She blushed, he snickered, and I felt torn between admiring his wit and sympathizing with her embarrassment. In the changing room, utterly unlike the musty private cubicles at Goodland's pool, the boys compared the progress of pubic hair. One older boy suggested that shaving the wispy beginnings would soon increase growth. Out in the pool, Jack, the instructor, ruthlessly told us all to get our heads under water and began teaching us the surface dive. El Reno would be different, but then I was different too.

During this astonishing summer we all came to know Dr. Morse better. He and Helene took a long car trip that included his family in Chicago, Dean and Faye in Atwood, and the newly settled family in El Reno. They arrived in their convertible, top down, basking in the June sunlight. Bob, as we were soon calling him, proved lively company, interested in everything about us, and far more engaged in public affairs than we tended to be. As we listened to the Republican nominating convention on the day Herbert Hoover spoke, the announcer mused that Hoover might stampede the convention and win the nomination. "That will never happen," Bob scoffed.

He seemed to relate effortlessly to all Helene's siblings. A surviving photograph taken in El Reno that summer shows him with his arm around a demure-looking Ruth, while on his other side, I lean against him, obviously pleased at the companionship. With Helene's instruction, we learned to distinguish between psychiatrist and psychoanalyst, and took pride in Bob's ascent to the more exclusive profession.

Best of all, Helene seemed deeply happy. Her one dispute with Mother blew over quickly. Mother had echoed the official Daughters of the American Revolution explanation for barring Marian Anderson from singing in Constitution Hall (that it was never open to such performances). Helene, coming directly from the scene, retorted that the hall was in fact the one auditorium in Washington where such large-audience concerts could be held. Any disagreement within the family stirred my anxiety, and this one pitted my pride in our Revolutionary ancestor against my budding sense of interracial decency. But on the whole this family reunion in El Reno left me reassured and happy. Helene's pregnancy seemed only to heighten her characteristic cheerfulness and good health. Looking later at a snapshot of Helene and Faye taken on this 1940 trip, I recognized the sisterhood of soon-to-be-mothers.

Although the move to El Reno might have seemed enough undertaking for one year, to say nothing of expense, my parents decided that after settling in we would attend the World's Fair in New York. We knew a lot about the fair and its theme, "The World of Tomorrow," from publicity at its opening in 1939. Generally acclaimed a triumph, it was held over for a second year, but I could hardly believe that we would get to see it.

Clearly, the folks were feeling more economically confident. Two of their children had married, and Ruth would not have college room-and-board expenses. Having bid in to be night chief dispatcher, my father was earning more. In the Rock Island timetable he brought home, his name appeared on the list of officials, though at the very bottom. The fair alone might not have justified the trip, but we would also get to visit Dad's sister Ruth, a district health nurse in Maine, as well as Bob and Helene in their Washington, D.C., home.

Dad planned the trip brilliantly. Since we were allowed only one eastward trip on a foreign pass per year, he designed a circular itinerary with Augusta, Maine, as its declared destination. That way we could spend time in New York and return through Washington, D.C., taking the Southern Railway on to Memphis, where the Rock Island picked up. Best of all, he had discovered from a fellow Rock Islander that our passes would let us ride down the Hudson River from Albany to New York on a passenger boat, which, surprising though it seemed, was owned by one of the railroads.

Never having been on so much as a rowboat, I delighted in the river voyage. After investigating the vessel's ingenious design, I settled down next to the guide, who sat with his microphone at the front of the boat. This pleasant young fellow, a model of Eastern suavity, seemed to know everything and to enjoy the cluster of young admirers who gathered near him. Of the sights he pointed out, only the soaring gray battlements of West Point proved lastingly memorable, but one verbal exchange has remained vivid.

The youngsters near the guide included one who, though speaking perfectly good English, identified himself as Italian. "And what do you think of Signore Mussolini?" the guide asked. After a calculating pause: "Oh, he's not for me. Too fat. Too much spaghetti." This appeared to be nothing more than lively banter, but Mother, who happened to overhear it, later explained that undoubtedly the guide was testing the boy's loyalties, given Italy's recent invasion of France. False though her interpretation may have been, this look below the surface of uttered words made the matter unforgettable.

Disembarking at dusk in New York, we found ourselves in a great gloomy, covered dock, holding tight to each other

We heard a lot about the World's Fair, but didn't imagine we could go. Author's collection.

in the near-chaos of passengers and luggage. If not quite the classic immigrant scene, it was enough to intimidate me, and I could draw on none of the confidence I had developed in railroad stations. Somehow we worked our way out of the jumble and found a taxi to take us to the New Yorker Hotel.

Having admired magazine ads for this hotel, Rena and I found it wonderful actually to feel the sturdy fabric of the lobby upholsteries. After negotiations that made us cringe, Dad got a good price for a room in which all five Hawkinses could sleep. I had no complaints about my narrow cot. It was reassuring amid the urban strangeness to have all the family together in one room. In any case, each day at the fair left me so tired that the hotel came to seem nothing more than shelter and sleeping quarters.

From the train that took us out to the embarrassingly named Flushing Meadows, I saw a huge cemetery with gravestones squeezed up against each other. Such disrespect for the dead would not, I knew, be tolerated back home, where graves were surrounded by grass and trees, with plenty of space to bring in flowers on Memorial Day. But I cheered up when we made out the much-photographed trylon and perisphere. We already knew that one stood for human aspiration and the other for world unity. Such unity was not much in evidence in this first year of World War II, and several of the European pavilions had closed.

Happily, the Finnish pavilion remained open, and we made sure to visit it. We had a high opinion of Finland, the only nation, Rena had learned in school, to fully repay its World War I debt to the United States. But did we eat there? Wherever it was, the memorable moment came when, tasting the dessert she had ordered, Mother asked the waitress what gave this cake its unusual flavor. The waitress whispered almost conspiratorially, "Rum." With reassuring aplomb, Mother nodded and kept on eating.

Displays of the new wonders designed for modern kitchens are a blur, but I distinctly remember Democracity, a vast diorama showing our ideal future in the World of Tomorrow. Happy to be sitting down after so much walking, I resisted the impulse to fall asleep. The green belt around the futuristic city included pleasantly sanitized versions of our Kansas relatives' farms. Most impressive of all, the superhighways showed how, by curving right onto a "cloverleaf" in order to go left, drivers could avoid the delay and risk of the usual left turn.

We went next to an exhibit that promised to show us real television. To demonstrate this technological miracle, two members of the audience were chosen to go into the studio while the others stood watching the screen. As the youngest of the group I was invited to do this, along with a beautiful young woman who said she was from Wisconsin. In the brief interview, I answered without stage fright, then gratefully returned from under the searing lamps. My family was smiling when I rejoined them. Yes, they had seen me, and yes, I had done well.

If the producers sought converts to the new medium, they failed in our case. Not until 1960, when their children presented them a TV set for their fiftieth anniversary, did my parents have a television in their home.

We were not used to swimming in an ocean of strangers, and the mix of skin colors, body shapes, and clothing styles far exceeded anything seen on the streets of Topeka, let alone Goodland. When a friendly boy, a little younger than I was, chatted with me as we waited for the band concert to start and then gave me one of his wrapped hard candies, I followed standard instructions about taking nothing from a stranger and put it in my pocket, not my mouth. As we left, I asked Mother if I could eat the candy. Wasting anything troubled her. She hesitated. "Oh, there's probably nothing wrong with it, but better to throw it away." Unprotesting though reluctant, I tossed it into a trash basket.

My parents and their two older daughters often referred to how much they had liked Boston when they had attended the Eddy family reunion there in 1930. To my disappointment, I barely glimpsed the city as we hurried in a taxi from South Station to North Station to catch the train for Maine. My aunt had arranged for a cabin on Portage Lake, far to the north, almost in Canada, and we spent a week exploring woods and water.

We saw logs floating down to a sawmill and daredevil loggers controlling the mass with long spikes. Dad caught a rainbow trout, exquisitely colored, and big enough that everybody could have a taste. The women lauded this manful conquest. Mother borrowed an old bathing suit and took a dip, an event indelible in family memory because she and Ruth, smiling in their wet suits, were captured in a photograph. It served to remind us that Mother, for all her prized dignity, had a playful side.

Aunt Lucy, as we called her, took that snapshot. Another district health nurse, she had been Aunt Ruth's dearest friend from nursing school days onward. She came from Massachusetts, from Worcester, the name of which she taught us to pronounce correctly. Her fascinating Yankee accent and her bubbly self-assurance made her a family favorite.

With no one else my age at the camp, I tried to entertain myself. I had never had a pet of my own, but here I captured a yellow and black caterpillar, which I named "Fuzzy." I carefully put grass and leaves in a jar to provide it a domicile. Occasionally I let it out to crawl about, and I didn't mind its crawling on me. The first two days went fine, but on the third morning Fuzzy lay curled and still amid the greenery. Here was death at its most intimate. I cried visibly enough that the aunts tried to comfort me. Caterpillars, they said, are not given to long lives.

Sad though I was, I might have forgotten the death of Fuzzy had it not been for some overheard adult conversation that afternoon. Aunt Lucy reminded my mother that Hollywood was looking for a young boy to play the lead in the movie version of *The Yearling*. "You saw how upset Hughie was over his pet," she mused. "Wouldn't he be perfect for that part?" Wonderful Aunt Lucy! I was not a crybaby, but a potential movie star. Of course nobody followed up on the suggestion. I did, however, take special interest in critiquing James Jarman's performance when I saw the movie. With mature objectivity, I admitted he played the part well. He stirred none of the animosity I had felt toward Shirley Temple.

Because our visit to Washington coincided with certain historic events, I can be sure that we visited there in September, on our way home. We found the Morses sharing their Georgetown house with Bob's medical school chum, Zig Lebensohn. He not only tolerated the invasion by his housemates' relatives, but engaged us in the pleasantest of conversations. A bachelor, he struck Mother, in one of her more improbable fantasies, as a possible match for Ruth. He won my lifelong affection with two gifts, a desk lamp, which I admired and he said he no longer needed, and a pair of magnetized miniature Scotties, which, in spite of efforts to be polite, I had clearly coveted.

Ever alert to public events, Bob subscribed to both the morning and the evening Washington newspapers. "You can't help but admire Roosevelt's timing," he remarked, with insight I considered brilliant. "First, he tells of Britain's leasing us naval bases in Bermuda and the West Indies, and then after the papers digest that, he announces, '. . . and the price: we are turning over fifty destroyers to them.'" We were all happy to see aid go to beleaguered England, but we could still chuckle at seeing through the president's manipulation.

Bob and Helene insisted that the young Hawkinses must visit the Capitol. Forewarned not to waste energy climbing the imposing front steps, the folks led us through what I took to be a basement door. As if that were not disillusioning enough, I found the halls inside narrow and crowded. Observing the hubbub, I felt a little like Jesus discovering moneychangers in the temple. Shockingly, a young elevator operator pushed a mother and her two children off the elevator, calling to a sartorially elegant, gray-haired gentleman, "Senator Vandenberg, there's plenty of room here." This struck me as horrendously undemocratic, and I was not consoled to hear the mother explain to a tearful child, "But, Honey, it's only because he works here."

Finding that we needed tickets to get into the visitors' gallery, we proceeded to Senator Arthur Capper's office. We had long subscribed to products of his publishing empire, such as *Household* magazine, and the folks regarded him as a good friend of the farmer. Seventy-five years old, he had been in office for over two decades. I did not see him, but Mother was invited into the inner office to be greeted personally. She did not reveal that we now lived in Oklahoma. In her version of what transpired, a rather bewildered Capper peered across the desk and asked, "Now, just who are you?" Well aware of what interests politicians, she answered, "Oh, I'm a member of that huge Eddy family around Topeka."

With tickets in hand, we stood in line for some time before being admitted by a self-important guard to the visitors' gallery above the legislative chamber. Even without being able to hear much, I recognized that the scene below contained animated debate. From discussion back at the Morses', I learned that the issue of the day had been a bill to establish a military draft, something unprecedented in peacetime. If this seemed ominous to others, their reaction escaped me. I had little interest in the war and never considered that a draft might some day affect me.

In fact, I was less interested in the European crisis than were some of my young contemporaries. I didn't listen to the radio news or read newspaper stories, and, perhaps purposely, my parents talked little about the war. Once at Grandmother Eddy's, playing with the children who lived next door, I had to feign knowledge when they urged, "Isn't it great the way the French have pushed the Germans back?" This misinformation dates the encounter as May or June 1940. Later I marveled at the narrow escape of troops from Dunkirk, but only when I saw *Mrs. Miniver*, not at the time of the evacuation, about which I heard nothing.

I can distinguish this Washington visit from several later ones by connecting it to Helene's first pregnancy. Although excited at the prospective maturity of becoming an uncle, I was a bit jealous for my place as her make-believe son. Clearer in my memory than such sentiments is an argument between Helene and Dad. Offered an after-dinner cigarette,

Helene accepted and deftly lighted it. Forcing a smile, he quietly asked, "Isn't that bad for your health? Won't that be bad for the baby?"

"Oh, not if I do it in moderation, which I do. I've talked to my doctor about it."

I was horrified, not only at Helene's indulgence in a practice anathematized in our household, but also at unresolved tension between family members. Later I heard Dad saying to Mother, "I didn't want to make a scene, but with Rena and Hughie there I had to speak up." What was the price of entering this sophisticated urban world? Some day I might want to go there, but for the present, adjusting to the newness of El Reno was challenge enough.

I returned to Oklahoma with Washington, D.C., New York, and Maine no longer just names in a history or geography lesson. They lodged in my mind as settings for specific memories. I thought back on Goodland almost not at all. When my new classmates asked where I'd come from, "Kansas" seemed answer enough.

CHAPTER 12

First Year in a New Town

El Reno . . . (1,363 alt., 10,078 pop.). . . . Marketing,
flour milling, shipping, and transportation are the chief
industries. The main lines of the Rock Island Railway
meet here, where the railroad maintains district offices
and division shops.

—*Oklahoma: A Guide to the Sooner State* (1941),
pp. 228–29

O N THE WHOLE the new town lived up to our hopeful
anticipations, but shift of locale alone cannot explain
the better life I remember there. Much was changing in
me and about me—the stir of adolescence, the improv-
ing national and family economy. In the first year in El
Reno, before I turned twelve and before the nation entered
the war, I fixed in memory differences found in a new
hometown in a new state.

As I began the sixth grade, tall for my age and skinny, I
showed no hint of a beard and was blissfully free of the
pimples and blackheads that sometimes dismayed my sisters. After the folks discovered my nearsightedness and
invested in glasses for me, I looked even less athletic. But I
welcomed the element of safety in the childhood lore that
declared it a crime to hit anyone wearing glasses. Adolescent bravado and rebellion, in my case never severe, lay in

*Hiring a professional photographer for portraits of Rena and Hugh
in the summer of 1940 suggested a new economic confidence.
Author's collection.*

the future. My family's sense of right and wrong still meant
far more to me than the opinions of any "peer group" (not
a term any of us had heard).

Together the family explored Oklahoma City, less than
an hour's drive to the east, known in El Reno simply as the
City. We observed the state capitol and commented on its
lack of dignity, with no dome to identify it and jutting oil
wells disfiguring its grounds. This rugged materialism jibed
with aspersions on Oklahoma heard in Kansas. Still, nothing could dampen our confidence that our new home
brimmed with promise for fresh beginnings. I stopped
imagining that I could return to Herington.

After a few days in the guesthouse, we rented a huge hip-
roofed house at One Thousand Sunset Avenue. Rena found
her Goodland correspondents impressed by that address,
but in fact, the monster sat on Route 66, and the rasping of

trucks climbing the hill woke us up at night. Before school started, the folks had decided to buy a house. Although uneasy when I heard the seemingly exorbitant price of $4,200, I found that the move into a home we owned gave me a sense of permanence I had never felt in Goodland.

The newspaper ad, I recall, described the house, in the recently developed Hillcrest area, as "not built to sell—built to live in." In fact, the original builder, Mr. Davidson, had planned to move his family there, but he ran out of money, and the house had stood unfinished for a time. Its present owners, the Rhodes family, had taken good care of it. When Dad balked at the price, they agreed to leave some of their furniture, memorably a bunk bed in the small west bedroom assigned to me. This was the first room I had ever had to myself, but it lacked a good deal as a sanctuary. The door had no lock, and my father often used it for his day-time naps.

The woodwork of Honduran mahogany won my sisters' praise. The built-in cabinets in the kitchen with their red plastic knobs obviated any need for our old-fashioned oak cabinet with its roll-up door and flour sifter. A second toilet, located down in the basement off the laundry room, proved a boon to me as my sisters primped endlessly in the bathroom upstairs. They reveled in the built-in vanity with its three-way mirror, using such cosmetic implements as their tweezers for eyebrow plucking and their electric curling iron. The shower offered another new amenity that made the bathroom a place to linger, and in one corner a laundry chute expedited the dispatch of soiled clothes to the basement and served as a conduit for shouted messages from floor to floor.

Most of the basement was devoted to a large game room, which featured a fireplace (never used). On our first Christmas in the new house, Dad presented the family with a Ping-Pong table. My pleasure in the gift diminished when

I heard him telling Mother that this accession would help keep the children at home. Deciding I might master at least this sport, I played both Rena and my school chums. Somehow I could never control the forehand, and I usually lost despite spirited arguments about the scoring.

In the City, the folks bought, among other purchases, a maple bedroom set for Ruth and Rena with twin beds and a chiffonier that cleverly concealed a desk. The furniture I had grown up with all traced back to accumulations "before my time," and I had rather liked the implied stability. Still, I had to admit that the new furniture set off the girls' room handsomely.

We assumed the Rhodes's mortgage when we bought the house. A month after moving in Dad drove down to the savings-and-loan office and paid off the debt, drawing on his Investors Diversified Services savings. In a tone of utter self-confidence, he announced to the family, "I'm not going to live in a house with a mortgage." He had never done so, unless you counted the low-interest loan from an aunt that let him build the newlyweds' first home in Topeka. Of his various maxims, "Always stay on a cash basis" ranked among his favorites.

Holding to such a rule for themselves, my parents fretted over the financial difficulties of my brother, reported in dutiful letters and then explained during a visit to El Reno a few months after our move into the new house. The packinghouse had failed. Dean and Faye had moved to Denver, where Dean found a modestly paid but steady job with a trucking company as bookkeeper and lading clerk. The couple arrived, proudly presenting sunny, blond Norman, the first of my parents' (ultimately sixteen) grandchildren. I decided that he looked like me and was irrationally disappointed that he hadn't been named for me.

By the family's standard of efficiency, Faye outshone all the Hawkins women. Stacking the dishes after a meal was avoided since it made them harder to wash. This rule could complicate clearing the table. Faye, however, quickly performed the chore, balancing three plates on each arm. Not even in cafés had I seen such skill. But for my parents, dexterity was no substitute for careful economic management. Mostly out of my hearing, Dean obtained Dad's help in getting money for a down payment on a Denver house, presumably the prime motivation for the visit. Naive though I was, I caught hints of the older generation seeking to take control. It was high time, my parents declared, to have the baby circumcised. They prevailed, insisting that they themselves pay the doctor's bill.

Hillcrest, the newest residential section in the town, sat somewhat apart from older neighborhoods on a slight rise beyond Elm Street. On the toniest street in Hillcrest, South Ellison, all houses had to be of brick or stone. Our street, South Hadden, had been controlled by no such rule, though all the houses were of recent construction, and one—said to have been designed by an architect—quaintly resembled the English country cottages in storybooks. In any case, South Hadden, with its lawns of drought-resistant grass and its slowly enlarging Chinese elms and thornless locusts, shared Hillcrest's aura of rising prosperity. One of the few two-story houses in the block, ours added to its distinctiveness by an extended dormer and a yellow brick chimney rising along the south side.

One fall day in a local beauty parlor, my sister Ruth sat under a drier, thumbing through a woman's magazine, barely conscious of the chatter of a customer getting a permanent a few chairs away. Then Ruth heard the name Hillcrest and listened closely. The woman was telling about making calls in that neighborhood and spoke of the delightfully musical doorbells she had rung. A slight pause. Then she offered, "Those Hawkinses certainly do put on the dog." Her hairdresser leaned down, whispered a warning in her ear, and she fell silent.

Ruth gleefully reported the incident as soon as she returned home, and the family mulled it over. Ruth had caught the woman's name, "Mrs. Penney." She was, we discovered, the wife of a dispatcher who worked a day trick and thus not directly with my father. Dad remained noncommittal about his colleague's personality. Certainly there was no bad blood between them.

Never having heard the phrase, I had to be told that the idiom in question indicated pretentiousness. Was the implication that we had risen above our station by moving to Hillcrest? How could that be when another dispatcher lived in the same block and our next-door neighbor was a Rock Island telegraph operator? We didn't even have a doorbell! The charge, then, must relate to family behavior. Had my sisters dressed a little too fastidiously for school or church? Was our 1939 Buick a cut above the Penneys' car? Had Mother's formal bearing and practiced courtesy seemed off-putting? In fact, she had never met Mrs. Penney. Had our summer trip been jealously noted at the Rock Island office building?

Arriving in a new town still with two marriageable daughters, my parents, I now conclude, had deliberately elevated our standard of living, giving a touch of truth to Mrs. Penney's appraisal.

On the whole, we were amused, even flattered, by the chance to see ourselves as (some) others saw us. But I knew I didn't want to be thought of as "putting on the dog." That would be no way to win friends in the sixth grade at the brand-new Lincoln Elementary School. I had caught a subtle warning in the comment of one of my Sunday school classmates that I reminded him of a comic-strip character called "Big Words."

Luckily three potential friends lived close at hand, none more than a block away and all fellow members of the sixth grade, two from South Ellison, Wilma Matthews and Gene Marshall, her father holding the local Coca Cola franchise and his the Chevrolet dealership, and, across the street from our house, Dorothy Ward, her father a manager at the electric company. I doubt if I compared their homes consciously with those of such Goodland playmates as Joy Shores or the Amos cousins, who rarely entered my mind, but the contrast was sharp.

Without prearrangement, we Hillcrest sixth graders often found ourselves walking to or from school together, sometimes dawdling around the lake in Legion Park. Late afternoons or weekends, we might drift over to one or another of our houses, the Matthews's yard and porch proving particularly spacious and inviting.

Along with the sheer pleasure of getting acquainted with these three and others, I found myself gathering information about life in El Reno. In spite of Dorothy's epic tornado trip to Oz, I had heard little about tornadoes in Kansas and certainly hadn't worried about them. But my El Reno friends dwelt on this threatening force of nature. Hair-raising stories preceded the repeated claim that no tornado could strike El Reno. The town lay between the North and South Canadian rivers, and tornadoes could not cross rivers. But one young skeptic challenged this theory. How could you explain the fact that Union City, also between the two rivers, had suffered a devastating tornado? What if a tornado originated between the two rivers? Maybe one should stay alert.

When it came to legal alcohol, Oklahoma was as dry as Kansas, neither state allowing anything stronger than 3.2 beer. Ultimately, Kansas was to precede Oklahoma by a decade in eliminating prohibition from its constitution. But even in the sixth grade I encountered tales about the bootleggers, a tolerated presence in the county. When a candidate for sheriff was asked what he proposed to do about bootleggers, I heard, he answered that he would not interfere "as long as they run their business legitimate." (This, I learned much later, meant not selling to high-school boys.)

Besides comparing reactions to movies and radio programs and trying to imitate their stars, we Lincoln sixth graders took pleasure in appraising our teachers. Our regular classroom teacher, Mr. Bates, also held the position of school principal. We were quite hard on him, suspicious that laziness led him to have us correct each other's papers after a class exercise. We thought he might have done better than assign us to "answer the questions at the end of the chapter." Why did he so often withdraw to his adjoining office? Of course, a principal had extra duties, but could he possibly be taking a nap?

Mr. Bates suffered from comparison with our reading teacher, Miss Middleton, who came in for an hour each afternoon, eyes twinkling through her thick spectacles. Everyone in the class seemed cheered as she stirred our interest in the stories and poems we read and discussed. She even had us do some writing of our own.

Embarrassingly, all seven lines of a poem I created in that classroom come to mind. Its theme suggests a reaching out for intimacy in the rigid rows of screwed-down desks with their disused ink-bottle holes and their grooves to hold pencils. The little opus had a shaky scan, but a dependably monosyllabic rhyme scheme: "The girl who sits in front of me / Her hair reminds me of a bee." I had grasped the need for metaphor, but the image doubtless sprang from the easy rhyme. My hopes may have been high. After all, Robert Louis Stevenson's *A Child's Garden of Verses* was a classic, and Emily Dickinson's secret compositions had ultimately brought fame.

My history report showed more promise than my poem.

I picked Demosthenes as my subject, attracted by his persistence in triumphing over a handicap. Drawing on passages in *The Book of Knowledge*, I made much of his overcoming his stammer by putting pebbles in his mouth and his vocal softness by speaking over the noise of a cascading brook. My account ended with his recognition as Greece's greatest orator. Oklahomans strongly admired public speaking—by ministers, politicians, or visiting lecturers. Speech courses were popular high-school electives. I enrolled in all I could. Besides those, I took "expression" with Mrs. Fitch after school (given free, since she needed a boy to balance out her recitals) and earned a war bond for participating in the American Legion oratory contest.

Miss Middleton whetted our hunger for recognition by declaring us eligible for certificates from the local Carnegie Library if we would read—was it ten?—books in five different categories. Each Friday the period was given over to silent reading. She encouraged us to bring library books we had checked out, but for anyone who failed to do so, she provided a few volumes to choose from. I considered having to take one of these a failure of initiative. After all, trips to the library to pick out books from the youth section, on the second floor, ranked as an adventure, well worth the walk downtown even on a hot day. For the history category I read an account of the youths of American presidents, including such edifying boyhood crises as John Adams's realization that school, however irksome, was easier work than spading the garden. It crossed my mind that it would be nice to be president, a possibility, as was well known, open to every American boy.

As long as possible, I put off picking a book to fill the science category. I couldn't find one that told a story. From the sparse offerings at the library I settled on one that traced the behavior of ants, aided by page-filling illustrations. There was some benefit; the book encouraged me to observe the ants in our yard more closely. They seemed less stupid after I read the book, though I never saw any sense in their carrying dead comrades back to the nest.

I read far more books than the number required for the Carnegie Library's accolade. Despite an occasional warning, "You'll ruin your eyes reading in that bad light," and calls to "get in the kitchen and help Mother," it was generally acceptable at home to have one's nose in a book. Built-in bookshelves in the basement, designed to conceal the gas furnace, served to hold the long-forgotten books that had been stored in Herington. On the hottest summer days, when we all descended to the cooler game room, I tended to draw from the treasures on these shelves.

I found *When Kansas Was Young*, impressively autographed by the author, *Pilgrim's Progress*, and some lurid Gothic romances. *The House on the Hill* featured a conniving and merciless stepmother. Her domestic villainy made Dick Tracy's public enemies seem mild by comparison. Intrigued to find that the author of *In His Steps*, Charles Sheldon, was a Topeka minister, I asked Mother if she had known him. She looked sorrowful and solemn. "He preached my father's funeral sermon. I was six years old." I felt torn between pride in this connection to an author and regret at having made her melancholy.

A battered copy of *Lamb's Tales from Shakespeare* caught my interest, but I gave it up after noticing the prefatory comment declaring these abridgments suitable for the sisters of young men, who would be reading the originals. The brothers might, the authors magnanimously allowed, choose to show certain carefully selected passages to their sisters. I decided to wait for the original versions.

Mother, Ruth, and Rena indulgently let me challenge them with questions from *The Quiz Book*. One question left us all bewildered: "Of which two brothers was it said that the philosopher wrote like a novelist and the novelist wrote like a philosopher?" I found the answer at the back of the book. But it didn't make clear if this "William James" might be the "Will James" whose books on cowboys and horses I had spotted at the library. It seemed unlikely. In any case, the puzzlement proved memorable.

As various pieces of our sheet music lost currency and lay out of sight under the lid of the piano bench, I had to dig to find my favorites. The lyrics of cowboy laments, purchased long before by Dean, told heartrending stories of betrayal and death. After I managed to pick out a melody on the piano, it would run through my head all day. Usually I refrained from giving it voice, but I couldn't resist irritating my sisters by strolling through the house singing, off-key as always, "I've got no use for the women. / A true one can never be found."

The open music above the keyboard tended to be the volume 56 *Songs You Like to Sing*. I hung over this book, fascinated by the lyrics and excited to find that many included the original foreign language text, mysterious words in French, German, and Spanish. That the translations into English were obviously not word for word made the scrutiny all the more challenging.

The magic of knowing a second language struck me when Maria, a diminutive Mexican American who came to help clean house, was sitting with us one day as we ate lunch together. The radio was playing "La Cucaracha."

"What do those words mean?" Dad asked her in a hospitable, conversation-making way.

She smiled. "It's about the cockroach can't go any further because he doesn't have a cigarette."

"Does it say what kind of cigarette?" Dad pressed, surely expecting a brand name.

She had given us the expurgated version. Now she clarified. "A marijuana cigarette."

"Hmmh," Dad replied, betraying no surprise. The

nature of the drug was never discussed in the family. After all, any smoking was bad.

The folks' willingness to buy a radio fit with their new economic confidence, but a tale I brought home from school probably helped bring about the purchase. Mr. Bates had chided the class for frequent tardiness. "Now, the radio tells the exact time, so you have no excuse. Is there anyone here who doesn't have a radio at home?"

Defiantly, I shot up my hand. Not that I intended ever to be tardy, but teachers didn't know everything.

"Oh, well," he said, "your father's a railwayman, so you can always know the right time." In fact, our family venerated Dad's Waltham pocket watch, its accuracy checked every six months by a Rock Island functionary.

I relayed this exchange at home, taking pride in "your father's a railwayman," but not altogether innocent of the pressure for family conformity.

At Lincoln Elementary School most students went home for lunch. But a federal program, unknown to me in Goodland, provided hot lunches, free to certain students, twenty-five cents for others. I recall bosomy, aproned women behind the counter, jolly and motherly, who somehow concealed who did or did not pay. It never occurred to me at the time that this was a program to aid the poor. On certain stormy days, Mother gave me a quarter and told me to eat in the school kitchen rather than coming home at noon. I liked the idea, finding the atmosphere highly sociable, and such was the mix that I never wondered whether others at the table were "underprivileged." (Did the word even exist then?) Although starchy, the food was hot. Once or twice I carried a sandwich and apple in a paper bag and ate in the classroom—not as much fun.

Perhaps I failed to see the welfare basis of the lunch program because, along with my friends at Lincoln, I considered another elementary school as the one in "the poor part of town." Yet two students in our class, who mostly kept to themselves, didn't fit our conception of Lincoln's status.

Velma and Nola lived near the railroad tracks next to the junkyard, and we understood that one of their fathers worked there. They were cousins, we decided. They came to school in limp, dark dresses, and their faces seemed to us to need scrubbing. I can't remember ever having talked with either of these girls, but we did talk about them. Velma, somewhat older, at least thirteen, had a soldier admirer. His starched khaki contrasting with her nondescript dress, he escorted her along Elm Street in the evenings, when the air often reeked of cooking alfalfa from the nearby mill. I saw them together once from our car window, but it is a story Wilma told that keeps their memory alive. She had observed the two from across the street one day when Velma's little sister was trying to tag along. The mother had called out to the younger girl, "Come back here and let those children woo." We found this hilarious. None of our families used that funny, antique word. Besides, even if Velma was older, no sixth grader should be involved in a serious romance.

A different incident has preserved Nola in memory. Midyear her family decided to move to Anadarko. It seemed hardly to matter, but Miss Middleton and perhaps another teacher arranged an in-class going-away party, complete with a wrapped gift—a small purse. Nola appeared shyly pleased. I reflected that the gesture was generous-hearted and played along with the other students in looking regretful.

By coincidence my sister Ruth was in the classroom that afternoon, substituting for Mr. Bates, her only appearance in that role. I felt proud seeing her in a position of responsibility, and her gracious ways helped make the occasion appear genuine. Delivering a brief farewell, she concluded,

"I'm sure El Reno's loss is Anadarko's gain." On the way home Gene stirred general mirth by announcing, "What she should have said is, 'El Reno's gain is Anadarko's loss.'" I laughed, too, feeling uncomfortable. I was mean enough to accept the insult to Nola, but the joke made my sister look unsophisticated.

A sense of racial as well as class distinctions sharpened for me after the move to El Reno. Compared to Goodland's zero in the "Negro" column of the 1940 Census, El Reno reported 350. How could so many fellow residents have left me with so few memories? Did something make these black citizens invisible? They lived in what one verbally elegant teacher called "darktown." Out of curiosity my family drove through it during our first week in El Reno. That hot afternoon no one appeared outdoors. The streets were mostly dirt, the houses widely scattered, and the brick Booker T. Washington School lacked any visible playground or adornment. Negro students, we were informed, would attend school in that building from first grade through high school. Theirs was a different world.

The area was personalized for me by Mrs. Madison, who came occasionally to help with housework while we lived on Sunset Avenue. Of indeterminate age, she had winning good manners, neither bold nor obsequious. She agreed to come to our house with the assurance that we would "carry" her in our car.

She lived alone on a low-lying acreage, her house set off behind a stand of poplars. A bit of family anecdotage recorded the phrase with which she had first instructed Dad how to identify her residence. "I live in that weather-colored house," she had explained. This euphemism for "unpainted" appealed to my mother, herself given to euphemisms. Probably I was not in the car to hear this expression, although I did see the house at least once, but

Mother's repetition of the story and its hint of insight into the ways of these mysterious others captured my interest and fixed the comment in memory.

Although I had arrived in El Reno certain that we would be living in "the South," where there would be a larger black presence, I felt far more curiosity about what it would be like to live near Indians. My images of this group drew less from battle scenes in Westerns than from my set of books, a treasured gift from Helene, about Indian children that emphasized tribal distinctiveness. Different though their lives were, these children appealed to me, much as did the twins of various nationalities in the Lucy Fitch Perkins books. (The French twins, caught in the turmoil of World War I, ranked as particular favorites.)

In Grandmother Eddy's tales of her girlhood, we were enthralled to hear how she watched each year as Indians trekked from the church mission to their grazing lands north of her home in Wabaunsee County. Once a band had come by while her parents were away, and she and her brother had hidden in the sleeping loft as previously instructed. Thinking the house empty, a few of the men entered, their behavior observed through a crack in the loft floor. They searched for food, finding only some bitter prunes, stored in a large earthenware jar. As soon as they tasted these, they spit them out on the floor and departed, taking nothing. The jar, converted into an electric lamp, sat in Grandmother's living room, often prompting this story. I heard it many times, delighted with its undertone of childhood fear and its comic twist, with these others as the butt of the joke.

We had little idea what to expect from the Indians around El Reno. The chamber of commerce brochure extolled the Cheyenne-Arapaho agency at nearby Concho. Curious, we drove about the grounds there, observing the isolated houses and the large frame school building. Nothing suggested a living community. Why had two tribes been combined here? We never found out.

A bit later, when we learned that Edwin, one of the children of Dad's prolific Uncle Jim and Aunt Cora, held the principalship of the Concho school for Indian youth, we called on him. Afterward my parents dwelt on the solid nature of his government job, though I have a less positive recollection that he described himself as burdened by the unmotivated students in his school. After Rena joined one of the high-school pep clubs (the "Squaws" rather than the "Pepettes"), we heard about the talents of Indian football and basketball players, some of whom lived at Concho and came into town by bus. At first amused by family names like Bushyhead, we soon took them for granted.

In downtown El Reno a few Indians contributed to what we saw as local color. Dependably, one or two aged Indian men sat hunched on the stone steps at the front of the First National Bank, where most customers used a more accessible side door at street level. No matter how hot the day, they stayed wrapped in their blankets. First laughing, then puzzling, we finally decided that the blankets must offer insulation against heat just as they did against cold.

At the junior college in her history class with Miss Shanklin, Ruth was studying the uprooting of the Five Civilized Tribes and their wanderings that ended in Oklahoma. Rena and I soon shared her sympathetic view of the obvious injustice. We examined the map she constructed tracing the Trail of Tears. If local legend dwelt on the occasional Indian who had ended up enriched by oil under his land, we knew that that was not the main story.

It seemed to my family that the presence of Indians gave Oklahoma an attractive uniqueness, a special character among the states. After all, didn't its very name mean "red man's home"? (This folk etymology mistook the Choctaw *homma* to mean "home," but at least it did mean "red.")

Our romanticized view was sharply challenged by a local dignitary. We had gone out to the rodeo grounds to watch a powwow featuring circle dancing by young Indian men with bare chests and feather headdresses. I observed no facial expression, except perhaps boredom, and decided that their hearts weren't in the performance. Standing a bit apart from the rest of us, my father fell into conversation with a leading citizen of the ambitiously named nearby town of Union City. Apparently impressed by the man-to-man exchange, Dad took the trouble to tell his family what he had heard. The new acquaintance had declared, "Show me an Indian and I'll show you a thief." Elaborating, he had explained that with an admixture of white or Negro ancestry, an Indian might be honest, but the pure Indian was irredeemable.

Whether because of my books on Indian children or Ruth's talk about the expulsion of the Cherokees, I remained unconvinced by this pronouncement, but I had no thought of challenging my father.

Frustration being a great reenforcer of memory, my sharpest recollection of attitudes toward Indians involves my dashed hopes for a grown-up social evening. It all began with Tommy Paley, the shortest boy in the class, but also the bossiest. He decided we were old enough to have dates even if we were just sixth graders. During recess he plotted with a group of boys to select from the girls in the class; each of us was to invite one to go to the Wednesday-night movie. Ever the organizer, Tommy drew up a list, and we picked which girl we would ask. I would have preferred Wilma or Dorothy, but they were quickly taken. "Who's left for me?"

"Well," Tommy advised, "you can ask Louise Mann."

I did, and she accepted. We were all to get our parents' permission and meet at the theater shortly after six that evening. With so many participating, how could our folks refuse?

Mother looked utterly skeptical when I told her the plan. "Who else is going?"

I rattled off the names of children whose parents she knew.

"And who is supposed to be your date?"

"Louise Mann."

"You mean that Indian girl?" The darkest-skinned child in the sixth grade, with glossy black hair, Louise's being "an Indian" was quite taken for granted among our classmates. Her family, like some others, had rejected reservation life and settled into the town economy.

I saw at once that I had struck some firm barrier set deep in family history. No way was I to be allowed out of the house for such a scheme.

Morose, I settled into a standard evening at home. The next day, as soon as I got to school, I asked Tommy how it had gone. Four boys had appeared, he said, but only one girl—Louise. Since the whole thing had been a fiasco, I sighed with relief. Tommy put an end to that. "Don't you see? She had to pay for her own ticket." My first date was the worst of failures. Paying for the girls had been the essence of the plan.

The family rules about apologizing applied here if they ever did. I sought out Louise in the hall at recess. "I'm sorry. My folks wouldn't let me go."

She smiled comfortingly. "I thought that might happen, so I brought some money."

Surely my parents would have approved of her graciousness. But they might have interpreted the outcome as meaning that only an Indian family would allow its daughter out at such an age at such an hour, and it seemed better to keep mum. There was plenty of family table talk without my revealing this painful aftermath, and nobody asked me how it had gone.

Louise's generosity of spirit eased my embarrassment at the time, but the memory of frustration and disagreement with parental judgment never faded.

⇒ CHAPTER 13 ⇐

First Year in a New Town
and a Bit Beyond

Turn on the radio! The Japanese have just bombed
Pearl Harbor.

—Rena

WEEKS before school started the family had joined the
First Christian Church, a step my parents counted less
as a religious imperative than as part of establishing us
in a new community. Finding a church home would
help "keep the children in a good environment" (a staple in the advice from Grandmother Eddy to her descendants). In a residential neighborhood in the older part of
town, the church's Romanesque brick building looked
vaguely fortresslike, indicating far more local wealth than
had most church buildings in Goodland. Even so, it was
outshone by the Presbyterian church and the First
Methodist church a few blocks away.

At ten years old, influenced by the suspense accompanying such hymns of invitation as "Almost Persuaded" that
ended each Sunday service, I had decided to come forward
only on a surge of emotion. Mother would have none of
that. She and Dad had already joined, and at the first service Rena and I attended, Rena started down the aisle during the first verse of the invitation hymn. I hung back, murmuring an objection, but Mother with voice and perhaps a
slight shove told me, "Go now."

How disappointing to appear in front of the congregation next to Rena and hear the minister identify us as the fine young children of parents who had come forward the week before. It emerged that we were now members not by "confession of faith," but by "letter."

Reverend Pringle's sermons were so low-key that I might have waited a long time to be moved by the spirit. Still, I liked him. His white hair topped a husky frame that reminded us he had once aspired to a professional baseball career. He gave a fascinating account of abandoning that goal back in his native Iowa when he received the call to preach.

His sermons, even if they did not stir the blood, usually held my attention, especially when he unwound the complexities of a selected scriptural passage. He could even tell us the differences between the meaning of an important biblical word in English and the Greek or Hebrew original.

Though he followed his notes closely, he would sometimes yield to spontaneity. One gloomy Sunday morning after a night that had brought El Reno a rare street-icing sleet storm, he launched into a sermon stressing the evil of neglecting church attendance. He stopped, laughed, and admitted, "I certainly have the wrong sermon for you good people who made it out today."

That was far from the only time he brought laughter from the congregation. More unusual was the time he evoked an "Amen!" from the back row. Ill-mannered enough to look around, I recognized the shouter as Mr. McClain, a Rock Island conductor who was our favorite on trips between El Reno and Topeka. Well, good for him.

Besides agreeing at home in our appreciation for Reverend Pringle, we found Mrs. Pringle pleasantly surprising, unusually forthright for someone in the delicate position of minister's wife. We admired her self-confidence. She had refused the invitation from a stalwart of the church's

The First Christian Church in El Reno, though more imposing than the one in Goodland, proved just as friendly. Courtesy of the First Christian Church.

women's guild to join the WCTU. "I can't do it," she had declared. "Their pledge goes too far because it rules out drinking cider."

Ruth faithfully attended the church's Thursday night choir practice. Rather than sitting with us Sunday mornings, she entered the restricted precinct of the robing room and marched in during the introit. Especially fascinating to me was the huge-breasted Mrs. Albertson, who used her vibrato unreservedly in her solos. Ruth herself was occasionally the soloist. Although she had sung such favorites as "One Sweetly Solemn Thought" many times, she remained nervous about forgetting the words and kept them on a tiny notecard cupped in her hands.

The choir included only women. Ruth explained the reason: once, the director, finding no men at the rehearsal, had arranged the special music strictly for women's voices.

When two men appeared on Sunday morning, ready to wing it, they were firmly disinvited. From then on men who thought they could sing left the music up to the organist and the choir, though I occasionally heard some bass harmonizing as the congregation joined in the assigned hymns.

At Sunday school's opening assembly, squirming on the wooden slats of the folding chairs, I could exchange whispers with friends from school. I could also get to know children who went to schools other than Lincoln, like the Frosch twins. After the opening hymn, prayer, and announcements, we crowded into separate classrooms, grouped by age and sex. The other boys declared this the most boring part of Sunday school. I never admitted my enjoyment in responding to the discussion questions raised after the teacher's opening commentary. I hoped they thought I was just being polite.

"You're lucky to have Mrs. Duncan as your Sunday school teacher," Mother advised me. "She did course work up at Phillips." Phillips University, the Oklahoma college founded by our denomination, lay some sixty miles to the north in Enid. Some of its ministerial students occasionally visited as guest preachers, and church leaders commended it as preferable to the state university in Norman. Whatever the benefits of her college study, they did not prevent Mrs. Duncan from simply reading aloud to us the advice passages from the Sunday school teacher's guidebook rather than studying ahead and expressing the suggested message in her own words.

Perhaps others in the cramped basement cubicle missed her flush of embarrassment when she found herself too far along to stop reading the sentence, "Your pupils are too young to know the exact nature of Joseph's temptation." She read on even more rapidly. I caught the hint of forbidden knowledge and determined to consult our Bible at home as soon as I had time alone.

Guided by the concordance in the book's rear pages, I tracked down the censored passage. With heart pounding, I read, "Lie with me." That's what Potiphar's wife had said to the upright Joseph. As with the *Jane Arden* comic strip Rena had omitted, I wanted to examine the text myself. In both cases the words "too young" had motivated me. The Bible, it turned out, provided far more instruction than the comic in matters that I found increasingly interesting.

I gained new sympathy for Mrs. Duncan's predicament when I saw how nervous Mother became after agreeing to substitute one Sunday as teacher of junior-high-school girls. Her children shared her uneasiness. Afterward she reassured us. "At least I was able to get one idea across: have a place for everything and keep everything in its place." Pleased that she felt vindicated, I still puzzled over how this homely advice had connected to a religious discussion.

After the move to Goodland my parents had sharply reduced their club activities. Mother had "demitted" (a more respectable arrangement than resigning) from her Herington Eastern Star chapter, where she had been a leader. In El Reno, however, she accepted membership in the Past Matrons of the Eastern Star, a group of older women who had held the top office in their chapters. She also joined the Woman's Culture Club, for which, like other members, she prepared short talks on such gripping topics as "The History of Glassmaking." We heard summary accounts after each meeting. Fond as she was of clear rules, she particularly admired the authoritative decisions of the club parliamentarian, Mrs. Korn. With her increased social visibility, Mother decided it was high time to have a new foundation garment, and I was banished from the living room one afternoon during the fitting.

Dad had demitted from his Masonic lodge and ceased paying dues as soon as he left Herington. In El Reno he took us to at least one Masonic social evening, though he never became active in the local lodge. The event comes back to me chiefly by remembering Dad's uncharacteristic irritation when I let the shoe polish stain my fingers. "They'll know we polished our own shoes," he chided, shaking his head at my clumsiness.

With over twice as many dispatchers in El Reno as in Goodland, Dad found a rich field for his man-to-man skills. The American Train Dispatchers Association tapped him to head its local membership drive. Bolstering my hazy recollections are reports in the ATDA's journal, *The Train Dispatcher*, of a drive underway to bring the "Nons," or "free-riders," into the fold. Membership was not cheap: initiation fee $10, annual dues $31. Affable but insistent, Dad raised the local membership to 100 percent. Beyond that, he convinced many to sign up as contributors to the "Widows and Orphans' Benefit Fund," which paid $500 to survivors after a dispatcher's death.

The ATDA counted among the railroad "brotherhoods." Conservative compared to other labor unions of the day, members had long exerted strong influence on Congress and the Interstate Commerce Commission. Partly because of brotherhood lobbying, the railroad retirement system, which went back to the 1920s, provided far more generous payments than Social Security.

As a result of Dad's local leadership, the brotherhoods began to send him their biweekly newspaper, *Labor*. I never looked beyond the headlines, but its front-page cartoons invited close examination. I gradually realized that this newspaper's perspective on capitalists and legislators differed considerably from the desultory discussions around our dinner table. Though occasionally denigrating "big business" and "bankers back East," these conversations generally favored Republicans. Dad sometimes mentioned

Eugene Debs with awe, but he frowned on strikes and often spoke positively about the Rock Island management.

For some now-forgotten reason I accompanied my parents when they registered as voters at Mrs. Quisenberry's house, on the corner where Hillcrest began. For the pleasant, almost social, occasion we sat in her studiedly tasteful living room.

"Now, what is your party affiliation?" she asked, application form in hand.

Mother looked at Dad. They seemed taken by surprise.

"Well, down here in Oklahoma," Dad half joked, "isn't everybody a Democrat?" And thus they were registered.

I thought this made sense. Choices in the primary appeared far more often on the Democratic ballot. A few years later Dad confided that it was better not to register in your own party. That way you could vote in the primary for a weaker opposition candidate. I didn't agree or disagree, but wondered if such a policy might not risk getting a mediocre candidate nominated who would go on to win.

The approaching presidential election doubtless had reminded my parents to get on the voting rolls. The conventions and campaigns stirred my interest, too, adding another frustration to the category "too young." Bob Morse's reaction to Hoover's possible candidacy fixed the Republican convention in my mind, as did a witty letter to Ruth from our cousin Marjorie Shideler, written while listening on the radio to the final nomination roll call. Overjoyed when Wendell Willkie surpassed the required number of votes, she had no doubt that Ruth would also find him appealing. Indeed our whole family did. That shock of black hair over a boyish face and the reassurance of Indiana origins—all nicely promoted by *Time* magazine—proved hard to resist.

One stifling evening we drove to Legion Park and sat in

the car with the windows down, hoping a breeze off the little lake might cool the air. On the car radio we heard a harsh ranting voice declare, "James Farley should never be our candidate because he is a *Catholic*." Adult reaction made the moment memorable. That was a shocking thing to say, or at least to say in public.

The drama of the election mounted as soon as Roosevelt agreed to run for a third term. Wasn't that unconstitutional? No, not really, the pundits declared, undercutting forever the passages in civics textbooks about our "unwritten Constitution."

Waiting my turn in the barbershop down on Bickford Avenue, I watched as one local fellow showed another a flier, chortling, "Look at this." The two men shared the item as surreptitiously as if it had been a dirty picture, but then they let me take a peek. It showed a plump-faced baby with a mere wisp of hair and a look of pained surprise. The precocious toddler was declaring, "A third term? Well I'll be damned!"

In milder language I made the same case on the school playground. I had in fact seen Roosevelt during our visit to Washington. A friendly trainman had told Dad where we should stand to see the president's limousine drive him away from Union Station, where he had just arrived. We joined a cluster of people at the curbside. As it turned out, all I could distinguish was a waving hand in the backseat window. But in schoolyard arguments I took this encounter as a source of special authority. I announced to a bunch of boys who were discussing the election that Roosevelt's large hand symbolized his reaching out to grasp power, virtual proof of his outrageous attempt to remain in office beyond eight years.

Other Willkie supporters in the sixth grade were few. I recall only Roger Burns, not otherwise a particular friend. After he declared that he, too, was supporting Willkie, we strolled about the schoolgrounds with our arms on each other's shoulders.

The day after Roosevelt's victory I went to school in dread of the gloating from the other side. It turned out worse than I had imagined, especially because Roger now announced that he had really been for Roosevelt all along.

The brevity of my chumminess with Roger was not unique. Often, at the Rocket Theater for Saturday matinees, I would find someone I knew down in the front rows, and with shared popcorn and conversation, usually unrelated to what appeared on the screen, we would become comrades for the afternoon. Unlike the seedy Royal, the Rocket, recently renamed to borrow some of the appeal of the new streamliners, showed only first-run movies, and its neon-embellished marquee dominated Rock Island Avenue. Its interior, though larger and more elegant than my old haunt at the Sherman, in Goodland, offered the same comforting smell of popcorn-butter and varnish, wafted about by the air conditioner.

When we urged movie attendance on Mother, she resisted, saying she didn't care to see any problem plays, but sometimes she did go with Rena and me to an evening show. *The Grapes of Wrath* won her full approval. Several times after seeing it she expressed her admiration for the character of Ma Joad, especially her insistence that "the family's got to stay together," an echo of one of Mother's own imperatives. She counseled me that I must never lose touch with my sisters after they married. A man who knew that his wife had a concerned brother would behave more responsibly.

During that first year in El Reno no Thelma appeared, with or without bicycle, offering to become my girlfriend. Despite the aborted effort to arrange the movie dates, we sixth graders were not ready to pair off. Maybe something like that could happen in junior high school, a step toward maturity, which, to my delight, would begin in the seventh grade, taught along with the eighth in a new building only a block from the real high school.

For both Ruth and Rena, the story was different, and I shared vicariously the excitement of my sisters' romances. Within months of our arrival, Ruth in junior college, Rena in high school, each had developed a relationship that we identified as "going steady." For the ever-popular Ruth, this was less surprising than for Rena, shyer and uneasy about entering a new school. Both young men had come to El Reno as teenagers, their families drawn there by employment at the federal reformatory. This institution, a boon to the local economy, helped citizens take pride in their town, and most fears about nearby convicts were put to rest by repeated reminders that this reformatory held only "first offenders."

Though small, the junior college supported an active social life. For its women students' club the high point of the year was a house-to-house dinner party for the members, a five-course meal with each course served in a different home. Ruth offered to host the cocktail course. She bought tiny juice glasses for serving the carefully chosen beverage.

Although sequestered upstairs during the gathering, I wanted as fervently as the rest of the family for everything to go right. We removed battered, comfortable pillows from the living room and hid the stacked magazines that usually sat on the lid of the grand piano. Normally left flat, the lid was artfully propped open for the occasion. I hurried downstairs as soon as the guests left, finding that indeed some of the tomato juice, spiced with Worcestershire sauce, remained. Deliciously piquant, it paired perfectly with the miniscule brown wheat crackers. Those two tastes, intensified by my relief that all had gone well, have kept the memory of that evening reemerging over the years.

That social evening included only women, but from Ruth's reports we knew of regular opportunities for all the junior college students to mix. Unlike the high schoolers, whose building they shared, they were of course free to come and go as their class schedules allowed. No study hall for them, and certainly study was not the main use of their dayroom, a lounge where new friendships formed.

Among the junior-college students Bud Hardwick stood out. He had been student body president in the high school, had played football, and remained active in the Boy Scouts. He looked like an outdoorsman, thick-bodied with short-cropped hair and unclouded blue eyes. Not tall compared to many in the school, he was a bit taller than Ruth.

She brought something fresh to his circle. A certain elegance came naturally to her, heightened now by her year away from home in Denver. Though a Methodist like the rest of his family, Bud began coming to our church for some youth activities that involved Ruth, such as Christian Endeavor meetings on Sunday evenings. He thought of himself as a future lawyer, giving no hint of the ministerial career that actually lay ahead.

Bud endeared himself to my mother by his bold entry into the kitchen. The Boy Scouts did, after all, offer a cooking badge. One day he arrived with ears of corn rushed direct from the field. Another time he demonstrated his alcohol-free mint julep recipe. The slow simmering judged complete and the house filled with a pungent aroma, he poured the mixture over ice cubes in prechilled glasses. On that hot afternoon, even before the first sip, I found my hands and nostrils ecstatically refreshed.

We soon knew all the Hardwicks. Bud's father had come to the reformatory as associate warden, and though he believed that, not being a college man, he could never become warden, he did win that promotion. The family's government-built house, a forerunner of the ranch style and the biggest on the reformatory grounds, caught your eye as soon as you passed through the main gate. Mrs. Hardwick, short and small-boned, seemed almost too tiny to be the wife of this portly, erect, and self-confident man, but I observed no limits to her energy and ability to manage a family of eight children. In one way, Bud reminded me of my brother, Dean. As the oldest son, he too seemed overconscientious about living up to his parents' expectations.

When the two families began to gather for picnics, I fell in with two of Bud's younger brothers. We wandered beyond their yard to the lake on the far side of the residential compound and drifted about in a rowboat. I watched with mixed dread and admiration as they spotted a deadly water moccasin, forced it to the bank, and cut off its head with an oar. I only half believed their tales of swimming in the lake in spite of the moccasins.

Ruth and Bud's romance did not go entirely smoothly. One night, after they returned from a date, his car roared out of the driveway. Later I heard Ruth explaining to Mother that he had been upset by her response, "Let's just be buddies," when he spoke of getting serious. He did not stay angry long. Ruth took up an outdoorsiness that did not come easily to her, and the two often went hiking and sometimes horseback riding.

These memories carry relentlessly beyond our first year in El Reno. A few months after war broke out, Bud enlisted in the army air corps, and we all worried about his safety. We found comfort in the thought that fatherhood probably would protect Dean from the draft. That status, Dad told me, explained why he had not served in World War I, that plus the crucial nature of railroad work. In response to a worried comment in a letter from my folks, Helene, knowledgeable as ever, wrote that no one who had ever been a patient in a mental hospital could be other than 4-F (unfit

Ruth and Bill (then "Bud") Hardwick, soon after their hurried wartime marriage. Author's collection.

for service). Almost certainly, this was the first clear reference I ever heard to Dean's illness.

On his first leave Bud announced that he must marry now or not till his flight training ended. No one told me about this. One day, when Dad was away in Emporia, I came home for lunch and found the house in disarray, empty of family, with no sign of food preparation. In the bathroom lavatory, filled with soapy water, a washcloth drifted.

Mother had urged Ruth, "Do it now." Reverend Pringle performed the ceremony in his study, with Mother and Mr. Hardwick as witnesses. The newspaper account, which included no picture of the bride, reported them as matron of honor and best man. The couple left for their brief honeymoon without my seeing them, stopping in Oklahoma City, I learned later, for birth control counseling from a specialist, an inspiration of my mother's, who had long felt she became a parent too young.

My parents' reaction to their youngest daughter's steady boyfriend was, to put it mildly, more restrained. Forest Allen's family had come to El Reno even more recently than the Hardwicks, in fact the same year we had, 1940. His father, like Bud's, worked at the reformatory, though technically he was an employee of the Public Health Service. Although his family, which included two older sisters, lived just up the block from us, it was in school that Forest and Rena got acquainted, sharing several classes. Both played in the band, which entailed early morning practice sessions, appearances at football games, and trips to out-of-town music competitions. Before long they began walking home from school together, perhaps the motivation for Rena's giving me her bicycle.

Though originally from upstate New York, Forest and his family had moved to El Reno from Kansas, just like us. But unlike me, he had quickly picked up the good-old-boy accent of Oklahoma, heightening his natural congeniality, underlain by an ironic sense of humor. Tall, dark-haired, with a craggy nose, he looked older than most of his high-school friends. He regularly wore cowboy boots, making less conspicuous the extra thickness of one sole. Although he strode along as rapidly as his classmates, he had a noticeable limp, the result of an attack of polio when he was eight months old. Since President Roosevelt had suffered the same affliction and the March of Dimes ranked as a national event, I readily found a positive context in which I could recognize and admire Forest's determination.

Forest's father, a gruff patriarch and navy veteran, took pride in sailing and sponsored a unit of the Sea Scouts, in which his son participated. Rena joined father and son on some of their outings to Lake Overholser, not far away, on the outskirts of Oklahoma City. Mr. Allen liked to be called "Skipper" during their turns about the lake. This honorific, plus recollections of a favorite comic-strip character, made Rena decide that "Skippy" would be the ideal nickname for a child who would formally be "Forest Walter Allen III."

Since he had no siblings my age, there was little reason for me to visit Forest's home. But his mother included me once or twice in dinner invitations to Rena, and Mother tried to accept with good grace my exuberant praise of Mrs. Allen's cooking. I was used as a go-between, as when the two mothers exchanged something fresh from their ovens. Mrs. Allen always initiated these neighborly gestures, but Mother refused to return an empty dish. Mrs. Allen specialized in pies, Mother in cakes.

Tensions between the parents of this couple ranged from something as trivial as my mother's resentment of Mrs. Allen's delaying the arrival of our mail by chatting with the postman to a suspicion on the part of the Allens that my folks thought Forest's limp rendered him an unfit spouse.

This latter, I am pained to recall, was not altogether mistaken. Predictably, such obstacles only enhanced the young couple's attachment.

Forest graduated from the University of Oklahoma in 1945 through an accelerated wartime schedule. With a degree in business administration, he joined the Shell Oil Company, where he was to remain for his entire career. Ignoring her parents' warnings that returning veterans could force him out of a job, Rena married him shortly before VJ Day ended World War II.

I missed this marriage ceremony also, since I was away in Denver, staying with Dean and Faye. I had gone there to take summer high-school courses, hoping I could graduate a year early. Both El Reno and life in the South Hadden house had begun to seem painfully restrictive. I yearned to leave for the outside world, and college counted as the first liberating step.

Rena's marriage was for me less memorable than the celebrating at the end of the war. Even so, the war's conclusion makes a pale memory compared to its beginning four years earlier. On September 3, 1941, I turned twelve. The same week I entered junior high school. No recollections of either day survive. But I can clearly recall December 7, 1941.

Our telephone, centrally located in the living room, offered no privacy. Still, Rena frequently used it to chat with Forest, as she was doing that Sunday after church. Slouched on the davenport reading, I heard only the lilt of her remarks. Suddenly she turned to the rest of us in the room, commanding, "Turn on the radio! The Japanese have just bombed Pearl Harbor."

Although from vaguely heard news accounts I thought of the Japanese as cruel to the Chinese, I knew nothing about any "Pearl Harbor." Doubtless at Forest's house his veteran father recognized its significance. Rena's outburst

Their wedding day. Parental opposition could not stop true love, and Rena married Forest W. Allen Jr. just before World War II ended. Author's collection.

and Dad's alacrity in turning on the radio fixed my attention and stirred a guilty excitement. Here was something far bigger than the family's usual plans and worries.

The next day in school, I competed with the others in homeroom to share items from the suddenly important world news.

After that Sunday, our lives gained a new intensity and family expectations altered. Even as wartime fears tightened the family bond, wartime urgencies pulled us apart. Dad rarely got his day off and frequently worked overtime. Recalling World War I loyalty hysteria, Mother cautioned us never to criticize any government war measure. Helene and Bob opened their house to friends called to military projects in Washington. With Bud still in the army, Ruth lived with us at home for the last months of her pregnancy, and Mary Anne was born July 10, 1943. Rena took a job as a typist with the War Department, living with the Morses and working for a time in the still-unfinished Pentagon. The separation from Forest only intensified their bond, and after a few months, she arranged to be transferred to Oklahoma.

After school, a card-carrying "Junior Commando," I spent time in scrap drives, door-to-door war bond sales, and even training sessions with the Civil Air Patrol. In a school pageant I played Uncle Sam, welcoming our Latin American allies. I had to grow up faster. Not that I minded.

Afterword

IN AN AGE of self-reflexive writing, more and more autobiographers end by doubting the truth of what they have written. I make no such disavowal here. I believe my reported memories are accurate. Still, there are many reasons to moderate my claim, not least my determination not to put down a hodgepodge of sudden recollections about long-ago experiences. I wanted a beginning, a middle, and an end. I wanted to tell a story.

The forced move to Goodland, followed by a second, more welcome relocation, offered such a form. No doubt I have overstated my resentment at the first move. Surely I was happy to have the family together, though I don't remember being unhappy during the year in Herington with just Mother and Rena in the house. When visitors to the Fowler house asked how I liked Goodland, they heard in response that I missed Herington sorely. Even as I spoke, I felt a little guilty about exaggerating to win sympathy.

To write, "This I remember," and tell no more, appeals to me as a way of providing good primary source material for some future historian. As an author who hopes for readers, however, I have fleshed out specific memories. Much dialogue has been reconstructed. Though I can swear to the accuracy of "I'll tip my hat to a lady, but not to a nightowl." I am not sure which playmate was with me when we discovered the discarded grade books, but it could well have been Gene Lee Beem. Perhaps my mother was not standing at the kitchen stove when I asked her to give me a compliment for Rena—but she often stood there. In several cases, though I recall the name, I have changed it to avoid offending someone.

Beyond such conscious filling in and alteration, I have of course gained context for my childhood experiences from family talk over the years, surviving documents, and recent direct queries to my sisters, but I have tried to make the distinction between what I knew at the time and what I learned later. I was usually attentive to adult conversation, no matter what the subject, but of course certain matters were not discussed in my presence, such as parental worries about their older children. Still, I usually received straight answers when I asked a direct question, as I often did.

The flow of memories I allow myself in these pages reverses the way personal recollections entered my classroom teaching. Offended by the egotism or laziness that makes some teachers chat on about themselves, I usually suppressed memories that I could have linked to the current topic. Occasionally I would indulge myself. The surprising result of sharing such personal minutiae showed me something of how memory works in a lecture room. Students recalled these anecdotes both in their essays and in casual conversation long after the course had ended.

Reflecting on what I have written about my early years, I can make a few suggestions about why, at least in childhood, certain memories survive. I find, as expected, some of the explanations suggested by psychologists: novelty, as with the first day of school; repetition, as with Fourth of July reunions; and of course strong emotion—shame, anger, or the pleasure of feeling important. As I opened myself up to early memories and wrote some of them down, I discovered other determinants of remembering: verbal playfulness, such as antithesis, alliteration, rhythm, or rhyme; a lesson solemnly imparted by an adult; an anomalous, unexplained reaction by some older person, or any other puzzling matter that I pondered. More sensually, sometimes a memory came back through the smell or touch of a thing, or even more, of a person.

Because I began this writing as an expression, even a celebration, of memory, my original plan was to check nothing, research nothing. But it proved hard to break habits developed during a long career of gathering credible evidence to tell about the past. The few family letters that survive from the 1930s reinforced certain memories, challenged others, and revealed family relationships. After some hesitation, I have been glad to exploit these, as well as the manuscript memoir my father wrote in his eighties, part of which I have appended here. As my interest in railroad lore deepened, I discovered the historically oriented Rock Island Technical Society.

I looked up certain details merely out of curiosity. Who was the "Emily" who wrote our etiquette book? How old was Senator Capper in 1940? Ultimately I decided that inclusion of such details, and even the broader social context, need not distort my effort to convey a child's experience. Unsure whether the diorama I recalled was General Motors's highly popular Futurama or the perisphere's Democracity, I took pleasure in finding the answer through the rich literature on the New York World's Fair.

To my surprise, I learned after completing a first draft that the Sherman County Historical Society had published a three-volume history in 1980-1981, much of it devoted to family reminiscences. There, told by himself, was the life story of one of my former classmates, Dick Hurd, who comes back in memory as "Dickie." From the newly provided context, I came to see that whatever the sorrows and strivings I remember, mine was the privileged life of an economically secure town resident. A few farmers in the county, I discovered, were living in sod houses at the very time we drove out to see the "old soddy" as a historic relic.

The motif captured in the title of these volumes, *They Came to Stay*, highlighted, through its very contrast, the central role played in my recollections by the restless desire to travel and move on. My parents encouraged this desire, even as they strove to keep the family together. This theme applies to our lives in El Reno as well as Goodland. Happy though we were to settle down in El Reno, the imagined futures for the family's younger generation did not include living out their lives in a small Oklahoma town.

Perhaps, living alone in El Reno, the folks regretted having elevated their children's aspirations. Forest has suggested that my parents expected one child to stay at home and care for them in their old age and that they had opposed Rena's marrying him because she had been picked for that role. It strikes me as unlikely that for such a plan they would have selected their least amenable child, but perhaps he observed something I missed.

In my case, as I packed excitedly for college, I noted a distinct wistfulness in both Mother and Dad. A few years later, when I was clearly on my way to becoming a teacher and writer of history, Dad made the fanciful suggestion that I might return to El Reno and the two of us set up a real estate agency. Fortunately, they continued to enjoy traveling and found interest in the varied locations of their children.

On many visits to Washington, D.C., my parents could share some of the Morses' active social life as they combined two careers with the raising of four children. Helene worked as a reporter for *Newsweek*, and later as assistant to the news commentator Joseph C. Harsch. Bob became a leader in national psychiatric organizations. The American Psychiatric Association established the Robert T. Morse Award in 1964, after his death from a heart attack at age

The El Reno house at 1028 South Hadden seemed too large after all the children left. When the folks weren't traveling, they were planning a trip. Author's collection.

fifty-eight. Reflecting his concern for the public image of his profession, the prize honors writers who have contributed to public understanding of mental illness and its treatment.

Other visits led my folks to Dallas, where Ruth's husband, now designated "Bill" rather than "Bud," studied for the Methodist ministry, and, when his studies ended, to west Texas and New Mexico, where he ministered to a series of congregations. Although Mother complained that Bill's sermons always ran on too long, she and Dad admired his rapport with the men of the church. He gained a reputation for motivating his parishioners to build a new church edifice, and the bishop often reassigned him with this talent in mind. Although she sang in the choirs, Ruth mostly limited her church work to informal counseling and keeping her husband well and happy. Their longest-held post was in Ft. Stockton, Texas, where the social room of the new church was named "Hardwick Hall." They chose Ft. Stockton in retirement, and their daughter and two sons lived nearby.

Visits to Rena and Forest were enlivened as their brood increased to five. Perhaps Rena intended to demonstrate that the very size family Mother had often complained about was something that her youngest daughter could manage and enjoy. Dubious about this fecundity, Mother opined, "They should start using twin beds." Forest's rising career involved nearly as many relocations as Bill's. Shell Oil Company moved the family from Tulsa to Midland, Texas, to Houston and New Orleans. Forest's business success and the obvious happiness of the Allens' home brought a degree of remorse as the folks recalled their opposition to the marriage. "How could we have been so wrong about Forest?" Mother said to me in a confidential moment. For their retirement years, the Allens built an environmentally adapted home in the bluebonnet-rich hill country of central Texas, choosing a location roughly equidistant from their scattered progeny.

In my case, parental visits found me once in Chapel Hill, North Carolina, where I did my first year of teaching, and then often in Massachusetts, where I settled in contentedly at Amherst College. On one of these later visits, they announced that "since it appears you will never marry," they were presenting me with $10,000, the sum given each child as a marriage gift. Far more welcome than the money, of course, was the implicit acceptance of my life choices.

These visits did not include Denver, though Dad did go out once to help when an ulcer attack hospitalized Dean.

Granting that health problems of two of their four sons contributed to Dean and Faye's financial woes, my parents still disparaged the couple's failure to stay "on a cash basis." Tensions between the folks and their daughter-in-law increased, and relations dwindled to birthday and Christmas letters with checks as gifts. Dean died in 1952 from a pulmonary embolism, after a major ulcer-caused hemorrhage led to surgery. Ruth and I joined the folks in Denver for the funeral. Dad paid the remaining mortgage on Faye's house, and Mother adjured me never to lose touch with my fatherless nephews.

After fifty years of employment with the Rock Island, Dad received a "gold pass," which let him travel unrestricted on any Rock Island train. But passenger routes were already fast disappearing. Grudgingly, Dispatcher Hawkins and his wife began to patronize the airlines, though never forgetting that industry's role in the decline of the railroads.

Appendix

THE RAILWAYMAN SPEAKS FOR HIMSELF

THIS EXTRACT from my father's reminiscences, written in 1970–1971, tells of his move from farming to railroading and his meeting and marrying my mother. A full typescript copy of the document, "Reflections of J. A. Hawkins," is preserved in the Amherst College Archives.

Late in 1901 . . . interest in my responsibility seemed to develop. That year my bachelor uncles decided to take me with them when shipping cattle to Kansas City. [In the] transportation to and from Kansas City one [of us] with each car of stock for a caretaker was [required]. To be considered a man I suppose did make a change in consideration [and] affected my ego. Upon arrival in Kansas City the livestock commission men (middle-men) met our train and from there we were escorted to a fine restaurant for a dinner at our choosing, and I always felt that the amount paid then for handling and sale of the cattle did make a difference in the quality of the meal. Whether any others noted it, I have no way of knowing. After the stock was sold or the sale was OKed by my uncles, we attended a show (play) and then went on to choose four cars of stock cattle to be shipped back to the farm.

For three years my father and we boys took on the task of big business to the extent of feeding two carloads through to pasture time in the spring. The expense of some additional feed and taxes made it necessary [that] we have additional cash; [hence] my first few weeks of working on the [railroad] section [gang] at $1.40 per day. It was necessary to have [myself] as a minor released by my parents, being under eighteen years of age. Since I had three uncles in railroad service, I felt I had [the] responsibility of a man.

After three years of cattle feeding and the death of my father, the AT&SF agent, Hugh Bryden, after watching we boys cut frozen bundles of cornshocks from frozen ground asked me if I would study telegraphy with him, paying $10.00 per month and caring for six switch lights. After four months' study the railroad put in manual block signals [on] account of some expensive wrecks [caused] by mishandling of orders by trainmen. This required three block operators at all sidings. From June, 1904, in eighteen months I worked at sixteen different stations on the Eastern Division. At that time I took the agency at Lang station, just twenty years after Uncle Will was agent there, and his cash book records were still on file.

Earl [my older brother] had learned telegraphy with me and was my night operator. [illegible] he fell asleep and delayed [a] mail train in February. Rather than attend an investigation, he resigned and found work as an operator on the Rock Island at Holton, Kansas, where he attended Campbell Business Col-

Newly employed by the Rock Island, assigned to Bishop Station, the handsome fellow on the right set off one day to find new lodgings. Author's collection.

lege. I learned of operators' seniority, and rather than break in at [signal] tower places [?] before becoming a train dispatcher, I resigned and went to the Rock Island, August 4, 1907. [I] was sent to Bishop Station, first station west of Topeka, where the operator had been on duty for eighteen hours [because there was] no operator to release him, thus saving my taking the rules examination at once. The Chief Dispatcher, after looking over my application covering my service on the AT&SF concluded my experience would justify such doings.

Operators at Bishop had been boarding at either the Brickyard or at John [illegible]'s residence one block south of station. A few weeks later due to California fruit trains starting, an operator was put on nights and I took the day job. Operator Lynch, a discharged dispatcher from the Union Pacific just hired by [the] Topeka office of [the] Rock Island, was sent to Bishop. The boarding arrangements did not suit him; so he proposed I start south and keep going until I found a suitable place with room and board (as we had been sleeping on a cot in [the] rear end of the box car office).

I was lucky as, coming to the bridge across the Eddys' creek, their nice dog Yag met me and walked by my side up to the Eddy family home, standing between me and the door as I knocked. Mrs. Eddy answered the door, and Yag kept looking up at us, wagging his tail and licking his mouth as if smiling. So after explaining my reason for calling and telling of my work as operator at Bishop, she said, "We will try it," and [she would] allow the night operator to follow me during the trial run. Mr. Lynch was a nice operator and proved an able assistant in making our trial days a success.

The house was neat and the Eddys' schedule very pleasant. The family at that time at home consisted of Harry, Bessie, and Jesse. Quincy, the eldest son, was a materials department head clerk at Topeka for [the] AT&SF. Harry had worked under him as a clerk, and Jesse and Bessie, twins, about ten or twelve years [old, were] going to grammar school one mile east.

Rena Augusta, fifteen, was attending Washburn High [i.e., Academy] in Topeka and boarding with her aunt, Em Boyer, her father's sister, [and] only returning home on week ends; for some reason the first four weeks after we started boarding with the Eddy family, Rowena [Rena's actual name] did not happen home. But an English neighbor friend, Mr. Lee, came to the Bishop office on one Sunday morning to acquaint himself with the operator and learn how business was on the Rock Island. While visiting, he happened to mention Rena [with great praise] as a member of the family—to my surprise as nothing had happened in conversation mentioning [this] other member of the family.

Early one Sunday morning as I came out of my room (which was the room just off the living room), this Rena appeared coming down the steps on the open stairway in the dining room. I will never forget the pretty rosy cheeks and brown eyes, plus the lovely ankles on the steps. Of course her mother came in from the kitchen to introduce her daughter to the new boarders, and was I pleased at the gracious introduction. It was the first sure clue to our winning a permanent home while working at Bishop.

At once plans were changed so [that] Rena would be home each week end and further that I would be permitted to go to Washburn for her each Friday afternoon when I returned from work, using the dapple gray pony Daisy to make the trips, returning Rena to school on Monday morning, since I was working nights, only one operator being employed at Bishop at that time.

There were other boys who showed up on Saturdays and Sundays; fortunately they were known as friends of Harry's; but I was threatened by some when playing games. [Then] one night at a real social party a mixed crowd met. Quietly in a quiet spot at the edge of the Indian Hill [Farm] yard, two young women whom I had met at church and Sunday school, who were Rena's friends, mentioned that Rena had taken me over. This conversation [took place] while Rena had gone into the house to fetch out the ice cream and cake for the group. I denied any knowledge of their statement and they simply said wait and see, which I gladly agreed to do.

A few weeks later, Leo Dixon, son of Verna, Rena's [older] sister, had a [new baby] sister arrive, and Grandmother Eddy went to Severy, Kansas, for the occasion. While Grandmother was away, I was sent across the creek to Orly [a married older brother of Rena's] and Kate Eddy's home to stay. [Their daughter] Gladys, six, inquired of her mother, "Why does Jim go over to Indian Hill on Saturday and Sunday nights always?" To this day Gladys does not admit she was enjoying home life to the extent of feeling I was joining in the family circle as one of them.

[Given] the extent to which Rena and I were enjoying each other's company, Grandmother Eddy agreed that I could bid in a telegraph operator job in [the] Topeka yard. This was 1909, the year Rena was graduating from Washburn. I bid and won third trick. At [the] same time Rena and her mother seemed to have joined in our serious affair and mentioned to me that March 23, 1910, would be a date agreeable to the occasion of a wedding. So I in turn called on Dr. Finch of the First Christian Church in Topeka, where we had been attending—to his surprise that I was to be a part of the Eddy family.

At this same time I started looking for a house near the yard office where we might live after being married. The [house at] 913 West 4th Street, only six blocks from the yard office, was for sale. [It was] owned by an old family on the corner of Fillmore Street west of 913. After my getting a price of $1700.00 on the place (at 913), Harry had rented the Indian Hill Farm, where he and Lois, his wife, would live. So Grandmother suggested she buy 913

West 4th Street and move into Topeka and Rena and I make our home with her for that time. This worked out nicely until we decided on a house to build at 830 Lindenwood Avenue.

At about that time there were a few conductors bringing liquor in from Kansas City for a few of the switchmen in [the] Topeka yard. The special officer of [the] Rock Island Railroad gave me the list of conductors and I was to notify him when they were called at Kansas City on trains destined to Herington. After a time, when investigations were to be held, the Trainmaster C. I. Kerr [?] asked me if I would be a witness. I said no, since I was building a home in Topeka and would be working with these men. A short time later a vacancy in the day telegraph office at Herington was to be open for bid, and the officials came to me and suggested I bid in this day job and break in as a dispatcher during my rest days and vacation time each six months.

This was in 1914, when we moved to Herington. But not until we had purchased four places in Topeka through Ray Shideler, real estate agent at 10th and Kansas Avenue. Each deal proved profitable, and shortly after going to Herington, a retired engineer from [the] Union Pacific at Salina representing Investors Syndicate Company interested us in buying stock, both mutual and stock shares. Upon moving to Herington in a few years we bought 401 South C Street from Conductor Myers. This place [had been] built in 1898 by a Rock Island superintendent.

Acknowledgments

INTROSPECTIVE though it is, this book has drawn on the generosity of many friends. I offer thanks for a wide range of help, including reading of early drafts, insight into the state of American publishing, and well-timed words of encouragement.

Among others, this gratitude includes Kate Albrecht, Doris Bargen, Karin Beckett, Madeleine Blais, David Chavolla, Benjamin DeMott, Tilden Edelstein, Jan Freeman, Richard Freeland, Allen Guttmann, James Haskins, Ray Hiner, Lloyd Holbrook, John Lancaster, Martha Lynch, Suzan Maxey, Drake McFeely, Joan Nagel, Paul Nagel, Betty Eddy Page, Horace Porter, William Pritchard, Rick Richard, Walter Richard, Martha Sandweiss, Keith Schroeder, Marie Stover, Richard Todd, and Kim Townsend.

Rena and Forest Allen cheerfully shared memories with me, as did our late sister, Ruth Hardwick. Generous contributions to my collection of family photographs came from the Allens, Mary Anne Hardwick Alexander, Jill Hawkins, Thatcher Morse, and Susan Morse.

Again, as consistently over the years, the staff of the Robert Frost Library at Amherst College proved congenial, insightful, and expert.

My thanks go also to the staff at Texas Tech University Press, who proved that current animadversions on American publishing do not apply everywhere, and especially to

Judith Keeling, whose thoughtful editing has made the book better in countless ways.

The Mellon Foundation provided support for this work through the Amerherst College Emeriti and the good offices of Peter Czap.

Index

advertising, 17, 19, 71, 90, 138
African Americans, 85, 91, 106,
    127, 148–49, 152
alcoholic beverages, 82, 130,
    142, 187
Allen Family, 168–69
Allen, Forest W., Jr., 168–71,
    178
American Legion, 144
American Psychiatric Associa-
    tion, 176–77
American Train Dispatchers
    Association, 160
Amherst College, 178
Amos Family, 97–99
Atwood, KS, 120
automobiles, xx, 16–17, 51, 68,
    72–75, 86, 105–06, 109,
    125, 126, 130

Baptist Church, 48
Barrett, Tommy, 45
Bates, Mr., 143, 147
Beem, Gene Lee, 43–44
Big-Little books, 8–9, 78
books, 21, 40, 41, 58, 76,
    89–90, 92, 144–45, 150
Boston, 131
Boy Scouts, 14, 165, 169

Bryden, Hugh, 87, 182

California, 104–06
Capper, Arthur, 133–34
Carlsbad Caverns, 111
cartoons in magazines, 90
Cessna, Miss, 35–37
Chapel Hill, University of North
    Carolina at, 45, 178
Cheyenne-Arapaho Agency,
    150–51
Chicago, 126
Christian Church (Disciples of
    Christ), xviii, 48, 51–53,
    155–58, 186
Christian Endeavor, 165
Churchill, Winston, 73
Civilian Conservation Corps
    (CCC), 112
Clark, "Aunt" Lucy, 132
class, social, 64, 140–41, 142,
    147–48, 175
Colby, KS, 75
Colorado Women's College, 25,
    27, 117, 124
comics, 30, 90, 99. 141
cowboys, 90, 117, 146
Daily Vacation Bible School,
    47–48

Dalhart, TX, 123

Dallas, TX, 177

Daughters of the American Revolution (DAR), 75, 127

Davidson, Mr., 138

Dayton Family, 10

death, 22, 42, 85–86, 132

Debs, Eugene, 160–61

Denver and Rio Grande Railroad, 82

Denver, 86, 139, 170

diesel power, xx

Dodge, Jonas, 21

Duell, Grace, 38–40

Dust Bowl, 1, 65–66

Eastern Star, 159

Eddy Family, 22, 52, 59, 68, 74, 75, 106–07, 131, 184–86

Eddy, Elizabeth Ann, 18, 48, 59, 70–71, 107, 150, 155, 184–86

Edlin, Lela, 20

El Reno Federal Reformatory, 164, 165–66, 168

El Reno Junior College, 124, 151, 164–65

El Reno, xvii, 123–26, 136, 140, 142, 149

Electrolux vacuum sweepers, 88

Emporia Business College, 18

Engel, Mr., 33

Episcopal Church, 117

Estes Park, CO, 114

Euwer Family, 82

evangelists, 54–55

Fairbury, NE, 123

Farley, James, 162

Farming, xvi, 4, 32, 61, 73–74, 96, 106–07, 130, 181–82

Farrington, John Dow, xix, 71

Finch, Rev., 186

Finland, 130

Fisk, H. D., 26, 91

Fitch, Mrs., 144

Fortmeyer, Darle, 32

Fowler Family, 82, 86

Free Methodist Church, 48–49

Ft. Stockton, TX, 178

Furniture and décor, 64, 82, 86–89, 111, 138–39

Galveston, 112–13

games, 7–8, 11–12, 16, 32, 44, 60, 63, 79, 93–94, 97–98, 105–06, 111, 113, 126, 138–39, 156

Garland, Hamlin, 106

Gibson, Mr., 37

Goodland, KS, xi, xvii, 1, 5–7, 65–67, 95, 113, 123, 149

Great Depression, xi, xvi, 2, 18, 35, 63, 66, 118, 120

Griest Family, 51, 89, 125

Griest, Faye (Mrs. Dean Hawkins), 51, 120–22, 139–40

Hardwick Family, 165–66

Hardwick, William H. ("Bud," "Bill"), 165–68, 177–78

Harsch, Joseph C., 176

Hawkins Family, 4, 18, 21,

48–49, 61, 107–09, 110,
112–13, 117, 151, 181–82
Hawkins, Dean, 5, 14–20, 40,
51, 59, 61, 63, 64, 74–75,
86, 92, 105–06, 118–22,
139–40, 166, 178–79
Hawkins, Helene, 5, 11, 20–24,
60, 114–17, 134–35, 176
Hawkins, James A., xi–xii, xv–
xxi, 5–6, 17–19, 36, 43,
56–63, 66–67, 74, 75–76,
83, 123–26, 127–29,
134–35, 138–39, 147,
152, 166, 172, 176–79,
181–87
Hawkins, Rena, 4, 6, 7, 14, 22,
28–33, 53, 72, 91,117,
122, 124–25, 137, 151,
168–70, 172, 176, 178
Hawkins, Rena Augusta, 3–5, 7,
10, 16, 20, 28, 31, 42, 45,
52, 56–61, 68, 75, 77, 78,
86–89, 92–94, 122, 128,
131, 133–34, 145, 153,
159, 163, 172, 176–79,
184–87
Hawkins, Ruth (aunt), 127–8,
131–32
Hawkins, Ruth, 5, 22, 24–27,
61, 76, 91, 117–118, 124,
140–41, 148–49. 151,
157, 164–68, 172, 178
Herington, xvii, 5–6, 8–10, 72,
76, 187
Hetherington Family, 112–13
high schools, 11, 26, 32–33,
96–97, 168, 170

history, writing and teaching of,
xii, 18, 70, 143–44,
173–76
holidays, 12, 34, 61, 82, 107,
138
Holt, Emily, 27
Holton, KS, 182
Hoover, Herbert, 126
household appliances, 88–89
Hudson River trip, 128
hunting, 62–63
Hurd, Dick, 175

illness, xvii, 19, 30, 34, 63, 88,
103, 118, 178–79
Indians, 21, 150–54
Investors Diversified Services,
120, 187
Italian immigrants, 128

Jakey, Mr. and Mrs., 10
James Brothers, 144–45
Johns, Horace, 63, 89
Jones, Relda Lou, 26

Kansas City, KS, 181–82, 187
Kimmel, Mrs., 37, 81–82
Ku Klux Klan, 108–09

La Junta, CO, 110
labor unions, xviii, 160–61
Landon, Alfred M., 4
Lawrence, KS, 21
Lebensohn, Zig, 132–33
Lindbergh kidnapping, 76
Long, Huey, 113

Madison, Mrs., 149

magazines, 17, 90, 91, 92, 133, 161, 176

Maine, 131–32

Marshall, Gene, 142

Masonic order, xviii, 159–60

Matthews, Wilma, 142

McFarland, KS, 106

memory, xi–xiii, 14, 38, 39, 40, 41, 43, 61, 81, 102, 128, 134, 143, 150, 152, 164, 173–76

Menninger Clinic, 19, 115, 116

Methodist Church, 48, 176–77

Mexican Americans, 146

Mexico, 111–12

Middleton, Miss, 143, 144

military service, xii, 108, 166–68, 172

Missouri, 21

Montana, 111

Mormon Church, 112

Morse, Robert Thatcher, 116, 126–27, 133, 176–77

movies, 9, 47, 51, 75–80, 91, 117, 123, 126, 132, 152–53, 163

music, 20, 22, 54, 73, 92–93, 117, 146, 157–58, 168

Mussolini, 128

Nation, Carrie, 82

Nebraska, 123

New Deal, 90, 147

New Mexico, 177, 178

New York World's Fair, 123, 127, 129–31

New York, 128–30

O. K. Packing Company, 18, 88, 118–20

Oklahoma City, OK, 112, 137, 139

Oklahoma, 137, 142–43, 144

Olsen, Miss, 37–38, 42, 43

oratory, 144

Parker, Bob, 44, 45

Philippine immigrants, 83

Phillips University, 158

poems, 21, 22, 41, 143

politics, 4, 48, 108–9, 133–34, 161–63

Pringle, Rev., 156

Prohibition, 82, 142–43

radio, 17, 72–73, 146, 147, 170–72

railroads and railroading, xv–xxi, 2, 60, 62, 65, 67–69, 104–5, 147, 182–87. See also specific companies

Ratner, Rev., 51–53

Real Silk hosiery, 19

religion, 47–55, 87, 91, 155–59, 165. See also specific denominations

Rhodes Family, 138–39

Rice, Mr., 26

Robbins Family, 83–86

Roberts, Cherry, 78

Rock Island Railroad, xv–xxi, 67–68, 71–72, 104, 106, 123–24, 160–61, 179, 183–87

Rock Island Technical Society, 175

Rockets (streamliner trains), xix, 69, 71–72

Roman Catholic Church, 49, 101–02, 162

Roosevelt, Franklin D., 4, 133, 162–63, 169

Sandzen, Birger, 87

Santa Fe Railroad, xv-xvi, xviii, 68, 106, 182–83, 184

Schofield, Willy and Ruth, 112

schools, 1–2, 8, 17, 28, 30, 31, 32, 34–46, 67, 141, 142, 143–44, 148–49, 163–64, 172. *See also* high schools

Scott, Donald, 44, 45

Severy, KS, 186

Shanklin, Miss, 151

Sheldon, Charles, 145

Shell Oil Company, 170, 178

Sherman County Historical Society, 175

Sherman County, 66, 73

Sherman Sals, 26

Shideler, Marjorie, 161

Shideler, Ray, 187

Shores, Joy, 96

smoking, 54, 62, 86, 134–35, 146

Southern Railway, 127

sports. *See* games

stage performances, 11, 25, 98, 182

Sunday school, 49–51, 158

swimming, 21, 126

television, 130–31

Texas, 177

theater. *See* movies, stage performances

Tilly, Ardith Ann, 100

Topeka, 48, 145, 186–87

Tornados, 142

Towse, Ellen, 21

Tripp, Elizabeth, 12, 32, 65–66

Union City, OK, 142, 152

Union Pacific Railroad, xxi, 106, 183, 187

University of Oklahoma, 124, 158, 170

Utah, 112

Van Zandt, "Bud", 115

Vandenberg, Arthur, 133

Wabaunsee County, 150

Ward, Dorothy, 142

Washburn Academy, 56, 60, 185

Washburn College, 18, 20, 22, 56, 114, 115

Washington, DC, 132–35

Wearever cookware, 89

Whipps, Mr.

White, William Allen, 108

William Woods College, 21

Willkie, Wendell, 161

Wolfe, Thomas, 21

Women's Christian Temperance Union (WCTU), 35, 156–57

Women's Culture Club, 159

Woodring, Doris, 40–41, 44, 45

Woodring, Governor, 41

World Wars I and II, xvi, xx,

128, 130, 133, 134, 150, 166–68, 170–71

WPA, 1, 35, 101, 126

Wyoming, 110–11

YMCA, 114

Zabell, W. T., 8

Zarnowski, Miss, 1, 9, 34–35

The author and Texas Tech University Press are deeply grateful to The C̲H̲ Foundation, without whose generous support the book series Plains Histories would not have been possible.